MW00898258

CIRCUS MATH

WRITTEN BY

Will Starr

AuthorHouse™
1663 Liberty Drive, Suite 200
Bloomington, IN 47403
www.authorhouse.com
Phone: 1-800-839-8640

©2008 Will Starr. All rights reserved.

No part of this book may be reproduced, stored in a retrieval system, or transmitted by any means without the written permission of the author.

First published by AuthorHouse 9/2/2008

ISBN: 978-1-4389-0836-6 (sc)

Library of Congress Control Number: 2008907224

Printed in the United States of America
Bloomington, Indiana

This book is printed on acid-free paper.

Will extends his deepest appreciation to Perky Edgerton for her beautiful illustrations and to Ottilie Sanderson for her tireless design work. Additional thanks to the Plymouth Meeting Friends School community for its support of this book and a special final thank you to his wife Lise for her patience and caring throughout this extended project.

authorHOUSE®

WELCOME

Ladies and Gentlemen

· ·

Today you will begin a fun and fascinating journey.
This mathematical adventure will take you to new and
distant places across our country. Throughout our travels
you will be asked to help plan many important details for a
small band of traveling circus stars. Each of you will work
independently, and together, to master your circus skills
for our actual classroom performances at the end of
May. I hope you will gain a clearer understanding
of what goes into a small scale circus production
and enjoy the rewards of your own full scale
show at the end of our study. **Ready?**

Here we go!

Welcome
to the
Circus

STARRING

Grace A.	Dominic	Mimi
Alex	Evan	Julia
Liam	Nico	Marley
Moriya	Jesse	Grace E.
Ryan	Ace	Celia
Moxie	Brandi	Andrew
Skylar S.	Max	Skyler J.
	Liam	

Come see the show!

TABLE OF CONTENTS

COPYRIGHT: WILL STARR

☆ ☆ ☆ ☆ ☆ ☆ ☆ ☆ ☆ ☆ ☆ ☆ ☆

OUR
CIRCUS
JOURNEY

The World of the Circus
Introduction

LET'S START AT THE BEGINNING. When was the very first circus? How were circuses the same and how were they different than they are today? Read on to hear a few of the gory details about how the first circuses started.

The term "circus," featuring performing animals, clowns and feats of skill and daring has its roots in the Roman word "circus" meaning a ring or circle. The Roman circus, however, was not a very fun place to perform. The star performers were often eaten by lions or killed in combat. Originally designed as a sporting event where Roman soldiers could match their skills against one another in Olympian fashion, it quickly evolved into pure chaos with a great deal of killing. The crazier and wilder the spectacle, the more popular it became. It reached its gruesome height under the Emperor Nero. With the final decline of the Roman Empire the event disappeared, but some of its terminology and legacy has survived. Some modern sports can trace their origins back to the Roman arena—bull fighting and cock fighting, for example. Words like circus, arena, and coliseum are Roman terms to describe a place to entertain the masses.

> Throughout CIRCUS MATH you will find a number of these yellow boxes with orange dots around them. Inside will be circus web-pages for you to explore. Enjoy.

1234567891011112

Below are just a few FOR YOU
To sit down quietly and review.
So try YOUR BEST, do what you can,
And off we go to Circus Land.

1. 17 – 9 = _8_

2. 174 – 63 = _111_

3. 42 + 67 = _109_

4. 9241 + 434 = _9675_

5. 4076 – 287 = _3,899_

6. 1504 – 645 = _____

7. Every Saturday we will perform 2 shows. The first one starts at 10:00 a.m. The second one starts 4½ hours later. Exactly what time will the second performance start?

8. If Brandi bought 4 tickets at $2.50 each, how much did she spend in all?

9. Grace E. and Jesse are both learning to ride a unicycle. If they each practice for 2 hours a day, how many hours will they practice in a week?

10. If Ashley's routine lasts exactly 10 minutes, and she performs this routine 12 times a week, how many minutes a week will she actually perform?

11. Will and Ashley have both attended many circus performances in their lifetimes. If Will has attended 45 performances, and Ashley has attended exactly 17 more, how many shows has Ashley seen?

12. Each time we perform, the show will last 60 minutes. If we have 4 shows in a weekend, how many minutes will this be in all?

13. How many hours will therefore be performed in a weekend?

14. Our tightrope walkers use a great deal of wire in their performances. If Evan, Moriya, Ryan and Grace A. all need 10 feet of wire, how much wire will we be needing in all?

15. One time, and just one time, Ryan allowed Will to shoot him out of a cannon. He flew 100 feet through the air. Then he walked back and yelled at him. ☺ How many feet did he travel altogether?

16. Ace sure likes to eat ice cream. If he eats 5 pints a day, how many pints would he eat in a week?

Introduction · · · · ·

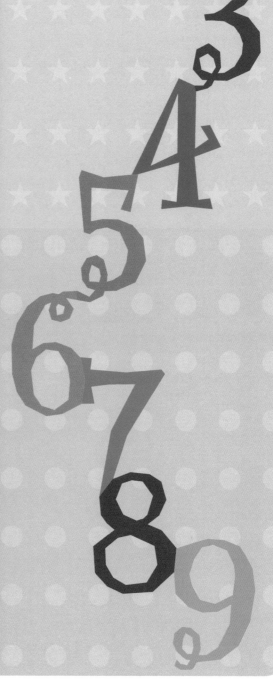

The term "circus," featuring performing animals, clowns and feats of skill and daring has its roots in the Roman word "circus" meaning a ring or circle.

Getting Started
Place Value and Review

THE DAY HAS FINALLY COME. We are all gathered at school with packed bags and high expectations. Though the air is clearly filled with excitement, a few of our performers are making this journey without their families, so sad goodbyes are quietly happening as well. Suddenly Will and Ashley, our two fanatical leaders, get everyone together to say a few things. They review with the troupe that we will be journeying around the country and be gone for the better part of the school year. In our travels we will see many new people, cultures and traditions and that we can all look forward to many wonderful days and nights of circus performances and parades. Finally, we are asked to make sure that all of our luggage and gear has been put onto the busses that will take us to our circus train, our home away from home for the next nine months.

Walking over to the bus, Marlena saw sheets of paper on the ground. Being the good environmentalist that she is, she picks them up in order to see what they are, and possibly recycle them. She immediately realized that these papers must belong to Will or Ashley, as they had charts of important statistics about our trip.

The charts had the following information on them. ⇨

Circus Journey 2008 – 2009

Performers statistics

Number of clowns	8
Number of stilt walkers	2
Number of unicyclists	12
Number of trapeze artists	17
Number of jugglers *(3 balls)*	17
Number of jugglers *(4 balls)*	3
Number of jugglers of other objects!	2

People statistics

Number of fourth graders in our group	21
Siblings that are joining us	10
Total family members who are also coming along	15

charts for the CIRCUS JOURNEY

Performance sizes
by numbers of seats

20 – 50	20
50 – 100	35
100 – 200	60
200 +	5

Shows

Total number of performances	120
Weekday performances	40
Weekend performances	80
Days with multiple performances	20

Money

Cost of each circus ticket	$25.00
Cost of cleaning supplies	$400.00
Cost to run the train	$1,000.00
Cost of food for the first half of our journey	$5,000.00
Salaries of staff	$2,000.00
Salaries of performers	$5,000.00

"Wow," thought Marley. I better return these sheets of paper to Ashley as they look pretty important. As she was walking over to the bus she ran into Moriya and showed her the cool charts. Moriya started to immediately read them and agreed with Marley that they better return these right away as their teachers would probably need the information. As luck would have it though they ran into Julia. She also wanted to see the charts, so Marley shared them once again. Julia though immediately began to think of the numbers on the charts and make up some problems in her head. (After all that is the kind of girl that Julia is!) She pulled out a piece of scrap paper and jotted down the following problems. When she was finished she handed the note to her friends and challenged them to solve all 8 problems. As the trio walked onto the front porch of the school, to get a little shade, they sat down and Moriya and Marley got to work. See if you can solve their problems as well.

Julia's SUPER SPECTACULAR problems

★ ★

1. How many performers are in our circus?

2. How many parents are coming along for the ride?

3. Lots of people like to juggle, like Evan, how many are able to juggle at least 4 balls?

4. Do we have more weekday performances or weekend performances?

5. How many family members do we have coming along that are not siblings?

6. How much money will the staff of the circus receive?

7. How much more money do the performers get than the staff?

8. Finally... how many tickets would need to be sold in order to make $200.00?

As the friends were finishing up the problems they heard Will say, "OK everybody, time for the picnic." As the performers started to make their way over to the farewell feast the kids and adults were chatting enthusiastically. Let's tune in.

Brandi: "I can't wait to explore parts of the country that I have never been to. Did you know that Wyoming is the least populated state in the country?"

Andrew: "Yeah, even little New Jersey has more people and it is a fraction of the size!"

Then we have...

Ryan: "I will sure miss my mom and my grandfather on this trip, but I am glad that they are here for this big sendoff."

Jesse: "I know what you mean. I will miss my folks and little sister. I will even miss my big brother Jason. He is such a nice guy!"

Finally...

Celia: "Would you like to ride unicycles together after we get to our first stop tonight?"

Alex: "Sure, I am working on riding backwards and could use a little help. Thanks."

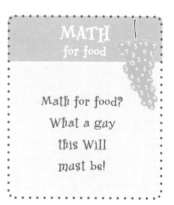

Math for food?
What a guy
this Will
must be!

Given the food that we are likely to be eating on this journey, everyone was very psyched to feast on the homemade food at the picnic. Mimi was so excited that she RAN through the parking lot to the picnic. As they walked through the gate that leads to the picnic spot, Will was standing there with a small sheet of paper. On it were 11 questions that he expected kids to answer before they got to eat. What a guy... I mean what a guy! A few of the problems had to do with food of course and answering them made everyone really hungry. Try them yourself.

They couldn't believe it. How crazy was that? Math for food? What a guy this Will must be. As they smelled the delicious hamburgers and the tasty dessert treats, each member grabbed a page and got to work. This is what they saw. ⇨

MATH
for food

1. 146
    − 31
    ‾‾‾‾‾

2. 345
    − 28
    ‾‾‾‾‾

3. 747
    + 216
    ‾‾‾‾‾

4. 809
    − 179
    ‾‾‾‾‾

5. 2097
    + 812
    ‾‾‾‾‾

6. 6005
    − 5197
    ‾‾‾‾‾

7. Each year we eat a lot of fruit on our journey. We ate 2,127 pounds of fruit last year and 3,974 pounds the year before. How many pounds did we eat in all?

8.   12 members of the class liked oranges more than apples. How many members of the class preferred apples?

9.   If each of the 12 unicycle riders has exactly $7.00 in his/her right front pocket, how much money do they have in all?

10.   All of the girls in the class get $5.00 spending money a week from the circus. How much money will one person get in a month?

11.   How much money will all 17 get in total each week?

After we each had a few minutes to work through the problems, sheets were passed back to Will and the feast began. **Cheers**.

The Picnic
Place Value Project

3 AS WE ALL WALKED OVER TO THE PICNIC, our mouths were watering over the delicious smells that wafted through the air. A wide array of burgers, corn on the cob, watermelon and pies greeted our hungry group. Before starting our meal, we had a Quaker moment of silence and then dug in! Well, at least we tried to dig in until Will stopped us... again. He said that we were going to do a little project with the ears of corn that were piled high on the picnic table. He reminded us that we have 17 ears of corn to feed all of the "pigs" that travel with us. Before we actually start our journey we need to make sure that all of us are properly fed and ready to go. Sure, we could just sit down and eat up those ears, which we will eventually do, but before we do, let's look mathematically at that corn. Let's answer these questions together as we compare and contrast our various ears of corn.

NOTE: New math vocabulary words will be written in yellow. No, just kidding, they will be written in green.

First of all, how many ears of corn did I say we have? _____

Now, without peeking, please GUESS how many kernels are on your particular piece of corn. _____

Now you can shuck your corn cob and ESTIMATE how many kernels you think your corn cob has. My estimate is _____ .

Why might your estimate be more accurate than your guess?

_____

_____

_____

Now, finally, you may count the kernels on your corn cob. How many kernels does your cob actually have? _____

Will your number be the exact same as your classmates, or not? Why or why not?

_____

_____

_____

_____

_____

Is this making you hungry? Don't worry. We will be eating the corn in just a little while, but first let's make a chart to compare and contrast your data with that of your classmates. Please turn to the next page and begin to fill in the information that you gathered, as well as all of the information of your classmates.

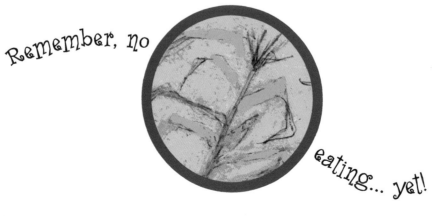

Remember, no eating... yet!

CORNY MATH kernel chart

student name	kernel guess	kernel estimate	actual number of kernels
1. Ace			
2. Alex			
3. Andrew			
4. Brandi			
5. Celia			
6. Dominic			
7. Evan			
8. Grace A.			
9. Grace E.			
10. Jesse			
11. Julia			
12. Liam			
13. Marley			
14. Max			
15. Mimi			
16. Moriya			
17. Moxie			
18. Nico			
19. Ryan			
20. Skyler J.			
21. Skylar S.			

Place Value Project

Let's take a look at our DATA to answer some basic questions about what we discovered.

1. What is the RANGE of guesses in our sample?

2. What is the range of actual numbers of kernels on our cobs of corn?

3. Which of these two ranges is probably larger? Why do you think this range of numbers would be larger?

4. Why do you think that estimates tend to be more accurate than guesses?

5. Can you think of another vegetable or fruit that we could do a similar project with? Tell me the food and then briefly describe how you would organize it.

As our circus train heads out we will be traveling west across Pennsylvania and into a new state. Somehow... somehow, its name escapes me but I will give you a few clues and maybe you can think of its name. It is directly west of Pennsylvania and its capital is Columbus. What state are we going toward? _____

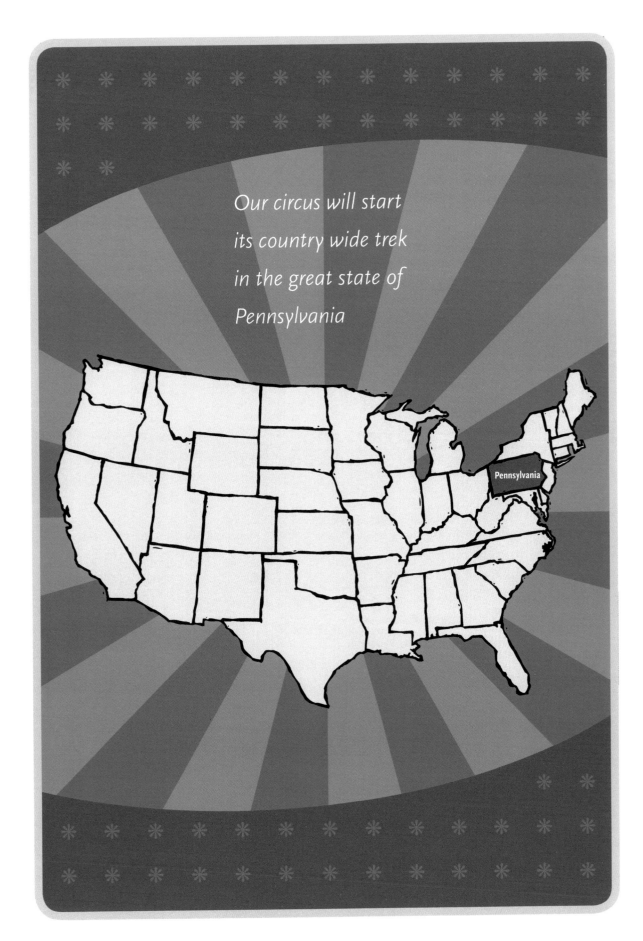

Our circus will start
its country wide trek
in the great state of
Pennsylvania

Pennsylvania

Back to our CIRCUS HISTORY Lesson

When do you think the first circus came to America? A man named Hachaliah Bailey claims to have introduced America to its very first circus. The story goes like this. One day a sea captain returned from China and had an elephant on his ship. Hachaliah bought the elephant for $10,000 and named him Old Bet. He taught Old Bet tricks and soon added more animals, taught them tricks and America's first circus was born. Hachaliah's circus would travel up and down the East Coast. He eventually decided that he needed a central place to winter the animals, a place that would easily take the circus to points North and South.

On December 16, 1837 he chose a location in Fairfax, Virginia, and bought 526 acres of land for $6,000. A long rambling inn, which stood at the crossroads, was improved, and barns and carriage houses were built nearby for vehicles. The inn's patrons were travelers, circus personnel, and drovers. Bailey brought much prosperity to Fairfax as people came to work for the circus. Whenever a circus was at Bailey's, the air resounded with noises weird to the countryside.

Hachaliah's contribution to the history of Fairfax, Virginia, can be seen today at the intersection of Leesburg and Columbia Pikes. The intersection is called Bailey's Cross Roads. Phineas Barnum acquired the Bailey Circus some time in the 1870s and dubbed it...

Barnum and Bailey's...
"GREATEST SHOW ON EARTH!"

Now let's try to answer the following questions

he taught Old Bet tricks

1. Who introduced America to its first circus?

2. How much did he pay for Old Bet?

3. If Old Bet had 7 brothers, how much would all 8 of them cost together?

4. Old Bet was an herbivore, like all his elephant friends. Take a wild guess at what each of them eats in a day?

5. In truth, elephants eat about 200 pounds of various vegetation a day. How much would one eat in a week? How did you get your answer? Did you multiply or add?

6. Old Bet would drink about 250 liters of water a day if he could drink as much as he wanted. How much would he drink in ten days?

Packing for the Trip
Fraction Concepts

1. Have you ever studied fractions before? When?

2. What do you remember about them?

3. Can you give me one example of how you use fractions all the time in your daily life? *Hint: think about going to the store.*

Try these...

1. Ace brought $\frac{1}{2}$ of a dollar to spend at the circus. How much does he have? _____

2. Julia has 6 quarters to buy a large popcorn. Will she have enough if a large popcorn costs $1.25? _____

3. Skylar S. and Moxie each have a $\frac{1}{4}$ of a dollar. How much do they have in all? _____

123456789101112

Now those weren't too hard, were they? Now, let me tell you a bit about us and who we are and how we get from place to place.

Our circus is made up of many different groups of people. We have performers such as the clowns, trapeze artists, jugglers and unicycle riders, but we also have many groups of people who are not seen, but who are an integral part of our production. We have people who are trainers and people who are in charge of lighting, transportation, and sales. When the circus crosses the country each of these people, and all of their equipment, must go along as well. Needless to say, transportation is a BIG DEAL. (That is why we have Nancy in charge.) We are going to begin our study of fractions by helping to plan and organize how these various groups of people will fit onto our trains.

ACROBATS
CLOWNS
DIABLOISTS
JUGGLERS
MUSICIANS
RINGMASTERS
TUMBLERS
UNICYCLISTS

Imagine, if you will, that the blue box below is actually one unit of storage. All of your "things" must be able to fit inside this big box. Therefore we will be giving this box a value of 1.

Let's say that you are a clown. What kinds of things do you think you will be bringing along in your box?

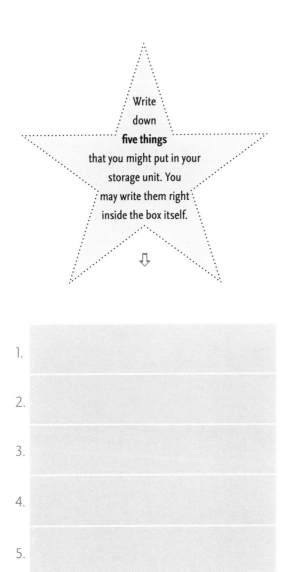

Write down **five things** that you might put in your storage unit. You may write them right inside the box itself.

⇩

1.

2.

3.

4.

5.

Hmm, what shall I put in my circus train box?

Now, I realize that this little box does not look much like a circus train, but for our purposes it will have to do. So, let's assume that each of these small squares equals the space in the storage car on the circus train. With this information, let's begin. ⇨

Max and his family are circus musicians who just joined the circus. As they got on the train, they were asked to share just one of these little square storage compartments. (Poor guys.)

Using the square below, try and divide it into **four equal parts**.

Please use a ruler and be as accurate as possible.

The dots on the boxes will help you divide your squares as evenly as possible.

OK, no sweat. Now can you **divide it three completely different ways**? Make sure that both examples give each member of Max's family the exact same amount of space. I mean after all, we want to be fair about this, don't we?

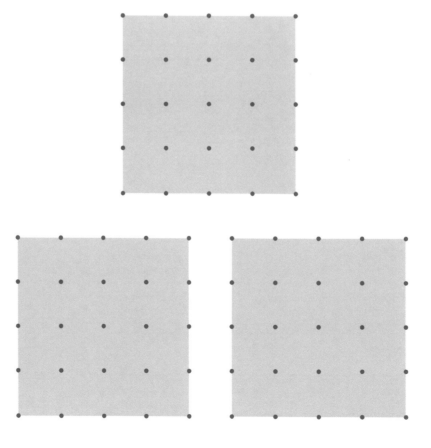

OK, ok. Now, smarty pants, I am going to give you six squares.
Can you now show me **six more different ways to draw quarters**? Ready? Go...

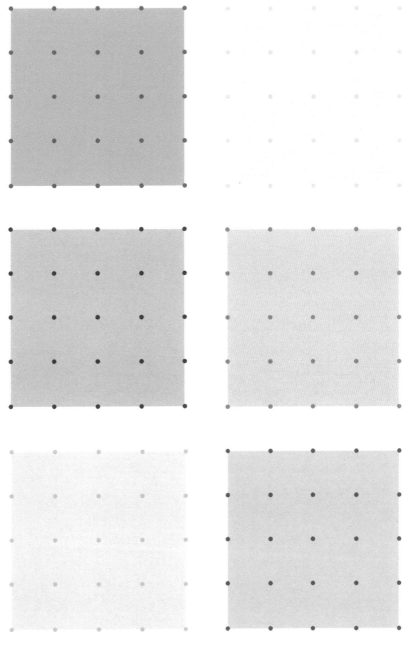

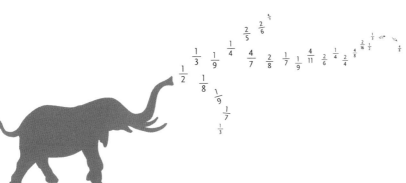

If Ali's and Marley's families join our traveling circus train, they will need to share the last available car. They will need to divide the car into **8 equal sections**. Can you show me one way that they might do this?

So, if dividing a square into four even pieces "shows quarters" dividing it into **eight even pieces** shows what?

How about dividing something into **six equal pieces**? What does that show?

What about dividing something into 73 equal pieces?

Can you draw four different ways that they can divide their space so that all **eight members** would get an **equal amount of space**?

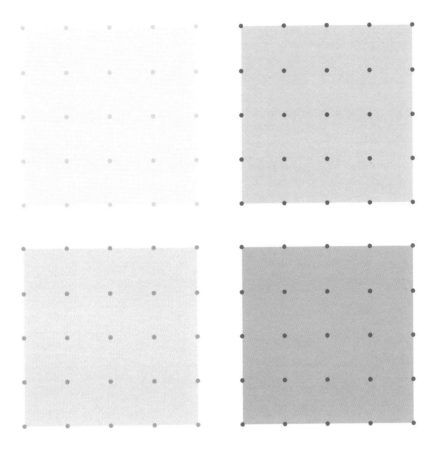

Hmm... What about 16ths? Can we divide this same square into **16 equal parts**?
Try to do it in TWO ways.

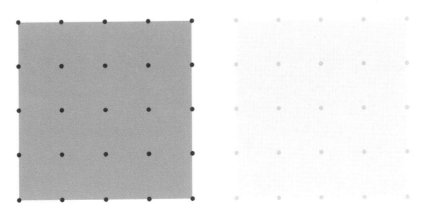

Fraction Concepts · · · · · ·

So we have taken our circus storage units and divided them first into quarters, then into eighths, and finally into sixteenths. I guess the larger the family the less room each of them has on the train. If my family has four people, Skyler S's family has three people and Evans's family has five people, which family will get the most room for each member on our train?

Please show me how you got this with your own drawing ⇐

Remember how we said that each square, or storage compartment, equaled 1? Now let's try to create some equations with fractions that equal 1. Try to show me the following equation and be sure to label each fraction piece.

$$\frac{1}{4} + \frac{1}{4} + \frac{1}{2} = 1$$

Fraction Concepts · · · · · ·

Try to divide the following squares into the fractions that are written above them:

1. $\frac{1}{2}$ + $\frac{1}{4}$ + $\frac{1}{4}$ = 1

2. $\frac{1}{2}$ + $\frac{1}{8}$ + $\frac{1}{8}$ + $\frac{1}{4}$ = 1

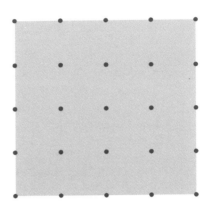

3. $\frac{2}{16}$ + $\frac{1}{8}$ + $\frac{1}{2}$ + $\frac{1}{4}$ = 1

4. $\frac{1}{2}$ + $\frac{1}{4}$ + $\frac{2}{8}$ = 1

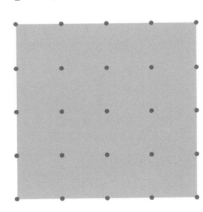

1/2 banana?
1/3 banana?
1/4 banana?

Now that we have looked at identifying halves, quarters, eighths and sixteenths, how about other fraction values? Could you divide this square into **thirds**?

Now, what about dividing another one into **fifths**?

Finally, how about dividing one into **sevenths**?
Try your best to do this as accurately as possible and to get seven fairly equal sections.

Before moving on, I have one REALLY important question. Ready?

Let's say I have two identical squares such as the ones below. If I were to divide the one on the left into thirds and shade $\frac{1}{3}$ of it, and I were to divide the one on the right into fourths and shade $\frac{1}{4}$ of it, which shaded part would be bigger? _____

Don't forget to use your ruler —

SHADE $\frac{1}{3}$

SHADE $\frac{1}{4}$

Now, can you explain why this is true? I mean, I always thought that 4 was larger than 3?

I am so confused, please help me, oh Circus Masters.

_____

_____

_____

_____

_____

_____

So, assuming that all circus cars are the same size, please answer the following questions

1. Which is larger, $\frac{1}{7}$ of a car or $\frac{1}{9}$ of a car?

2. I have $\frac{1}{2}$ of a car and Ace has $\frac{2}{4}$ of a car. Do we have the same amount? Why?

3. Ashley is very special and has her own car. Suddenly Jesse came and took $\frac{2}{5}$ of his car, how much would be left?

4. Finally, if Andrew had $\frac{1}{4}$ of a car and Ashley had $\frac{1}{2}$ of the same car, how many fourths would be left?

5. Finally, if Will owns $\frac{1}{3}$ as many unicycles as his friend Eric, how many cycles does Will have if Eric owns 18?

Back to OUR JOURNEY

ONE BRIGHT AND SUNNY DAY, as we were traveling over the Appalachian Mountains into Pennsylvania, one of the fathers got upset by the unfairness of storage. He said that parents should get a larger share of storage since they are physically larger. The kids naturally liked the current system, but agreed to talk about it. Our entire group of circus performers reached consensus and decided to change the way we all shared space. Please look at the following three equations and try to solve them given this new policy of ours.

1. Liam and his family of fire eaters all share a storage car on the train. Liam gets one quarter of the storage, his sister Eva gets one eighth, his dad Chris gets one eighth, and his mom Nicole gets one half. *Draw your own square and show me how this looks.*

2. Will and his mom share a car as well. Since they are both stilt walkers, they need lots of room for their long stilts. The stilts need $\frac{3}{4}$ of the car, Will needs $\frac{1}{8}$ and his mom needs $\frac{1}{8}$. How would this equation look in the space at right?

3. Jesse has one of the best jobs in the circus. His family drives the motorcycles in the Chamber of Death stunt. His family consists of his mom and dad, Laurie and Michael, his brother Jason and his sister Chloe. Since his parents do not ride the cycles anymore, the kids each have to store the three bikes in one car of the train. Jesse is given one quarter of the car, Chloe is given one quarter of the car and Jesse gets one half. How would a drawing of their car look?

Fraction Concepts · · · · · ·

As you can see, fractions are an important part of our traveling circus, and storage is just one small piece of this. Feeding everyone as we travel across the USA also involves fractions, and making sure each circus member is paid their fair share also uses this important tool. It is important that each of you understands the relationship between various fraction pieces. Before we move onto multiplication, please answer the following questions about fractions.

1. Grace E. eats $\frac{1}{2}$ of a pizza at each meal. Brandi eats $\frac{3}{4}$ of a pizza at each meal. Assuming the pizzas are the same size, who eats more? *Please draw your answer.*

2. Will can only juggle $\frac{1}{3}$ as many balls as Maya. If Celia can juggle 9 balls at once, how many balls can Will juggle?

3. Moriya, Moxie and Grace A. each practice for $2\frac{1}{2}$ hours a day. Impressive, eh? How many hours do they practice in a week? *Please show with a drawing and be careful.*

4. Jesse and Will's son Max are both really hungry, so during a break in performing they go out and buy 13 apple pies. If they split these pies equally between them how many pies do they each get?

13 apple pies

Fraction Concepts · · · ·

Our circus train begins to head southward

Fraction Concepts

AS OUR CIRCUS TRAIN BEGINS TO HEAD SOUTHWARD into Maryland, Virginia, and the Carolinas, each of us has some free time between performances to talk and play games. This is a relief for our motorcycle riders and fire eaters, as they naturally need breaks from their difficult tasks. As one would expect, our traveling circus train has many cars in addition to just storage ones and food cars. We have one car that is entirely devoted to games and relaxation. All members of our traveling group are free to go here to play or relax. Here is where Julia and Ace are playing a game that uses some of the fraction skills that they have learned over the past few weeks.

Let's check in on their conversation

Julia: "How do you play again Ace?"

Ace: "Take a word like battle. It has six letters in it. B-a-t-t-l-e. If I take the first $\frac{1}{2}$ of the word that would be the first three letters out of six. Right? So the first three letters can be pulled out to make another word B-a-t or BAT. We try to stump each other by saying a word and seeing if the other person can come up with a new word by taking out a small fraction of it. Get it?"

Battle

Julia: "Sure, let's try it"

Ace: "OK, what word comes from the first $\frac{4}{8}$ or $\frac{1}{2}$ of football?"

Julia: "That's easy it is _____. How about this one? What word comes from the first $\frac{2}{6}$ or $\frac{1}{3}$ of animal?"

Ace: "Hmm. I know that must be _____ . Here is a harder one. What name comes from the last $\frac{4}{7}$ of the name Abigail?"

Julia: "_____ of course. OK, one more. This is really tricky. What word comes from the first $\frac{4}{11}$ of the word mathematics?"

Ace: "Hmm. That is a long word. Let's see... I think it is... maybe, oh, I know. It is _____!"

Just then, Julia's mom Terry came into the room and asked both kids to head back to the train car as we were pulling into our next stop. This stop was the capital of Florida. Which was?

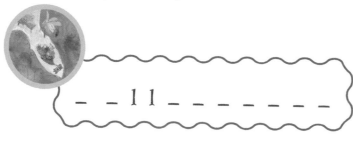

_ _ 1 1 _ _ _ _ _ _ _

Words that have words inside of them

Now, try a few of your own. Just like Dominic and Mimi's, try to come up with words that have other words inside of them. Feel free to use any fraction pieces that you know. A few good ones to try would be: eighths, quarters, or halves. You can also use thirds, sixths or even ninths for longer words. Remember that the numerator does not always have to be a one, and the denominator is almost always the number of letters in the word. Try to make up four different problems that we will solve as a class.

1. _____

   _____

   _____

   _____

2. _____

   _____

   _____

   _____

   _____

   _____

3. _____

   _____

   _____

   _____

   _____

Fraction wrap-up

If you remember, at the start of this unit, I said that fractions were not all that hard and I hope you now feel the same way. Before we wrap up this section of our work on fractions, try a few final problems to test your skills.

1.   Which is larger, $\frac{1}{4}$ or $\frac{1}{2}$?

2. $\frac{1}{4} + \frac{1}{4} =$

3.   Which is larger $\frac{1}{2}$ or $\frac{2}{4}$? *Show me your answer with a drawing.*

4.   Just before leaving the state of Florida, unicycle queen Celia tried to break the world car jumping record. In her three attempts she flew $4\frac{1}{2}$, $5\frac{1}{4}$ and an earth shattering $6\frac{3}{4}$ feet through the air. How many feet she did fly in all three jumps combined?

5.   Will sure loves to unicycle. Last week he rode each and every day of the week. On Monday he rode $\frac{1}{2}$ of a mile. On Tuesday he rode twice as far as he did on Monday. On Wednesday he rode twice as far as he did on Tuesday. He did this each and every day through a long ride on Sunday. Please tell me how far he rode during the week. *Feel free to make a chart or draw a table to help you!*

Will sure loves his unicycle

Math is Everywhere!
Fraction Project

AFTER A COUPLE OF HIGHLY SUCCESSFUL performances in Florida, we get back on the train heading NW through Georgia, Alabama and Mississippi. We are heading down the tracks on our way to a series of shows in Lafayette, Louisiana. Driving across the bayous we are reminded of the vast cultural significance of the area, from the original native inhabitants to the French Arcadians and of course the Louisiana Purchase in 1803. New Orleans, now a hotbed for music, food and cultural diversity, was a fun layover for our traveling circus troupe.

After our brief stop in the Big Easy we gathered all the performers together to work on a little project. Let's listen in as Will is explaining the details. ⇨

Websites about New Orleans:

www.neworleansonline.com

www.neworleans.com/kids

www.nojazzfest.com

1234**5**6789101112

> "First of all, I want to say what a wonderful job everyone did in the shows last week. You really wowed those Florida audiences and they naturally asked if we had planned on returning next year! I am also glad that so many of you got some time to explore New Orleans and try to understand the social impact that it has on our country as a whole, as well as work on coming to terms with the devastation caused by Hurricane Katrina. As always, you continue to impress me with your inquisitiveness and your outreach to others.
>
> Between now and when we reach our destination in Lafayette, Louisiana we will be working collectively on a project to make a paper quilt. My goal is to use the fraction skills and concepts that you have been working on, to build a beautiful quilt to hang in the food car throughout the rest of the journey. If we work together we can create a real masterpiece for all of our visual enjoyment. Sound good? "

Here is how it will work. ⇩

Step 1

"I have placed a wide variety of colored paper on the tables in front of you. Your first job is to choose one sheet that you like and wait for your buddies to do the same. Once this has happened you will also need a ruler and a pencil. If you place the paper vertically in front of you, take your ruler and **measure 8 inches across the very top of the sheet**. By starting with your ruler in the upper left hand corner, you can find exactly eight inches and put a small dot on that mark. Then, **do the same on the bottom edge of the sheet**, putting a dot at exactly 8 inches. If you then take your ruler and line it up with those two dots, **a vertical line can be drawn to connect the dots**. You will notice that this line is exactly 8 inches from the left edge of the paper. As soon as everyone has done that I will proceed."

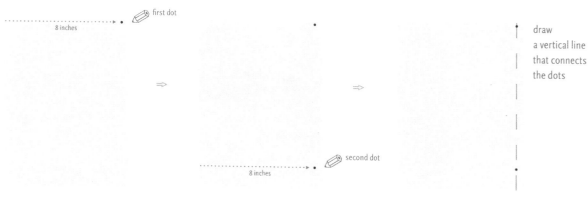

8 inches — first dot

draw a dot at the top

8 inches — second dot

draw a second dot

draw a vertical line that connects the dots

"Now, flip your paper 90 degrees to the right. Measure 8 inches on the new top edge of the sheet and **make a third dot**. Now, measure 8 inches on the bottom edge of the sheet and **place a fourth dot** there.

When you **connect these dots** you will clearly see that **you have constructed an exact 8 inch square**. This will be your square for our project. Carefully **cut it out** and again wait for your buddies."

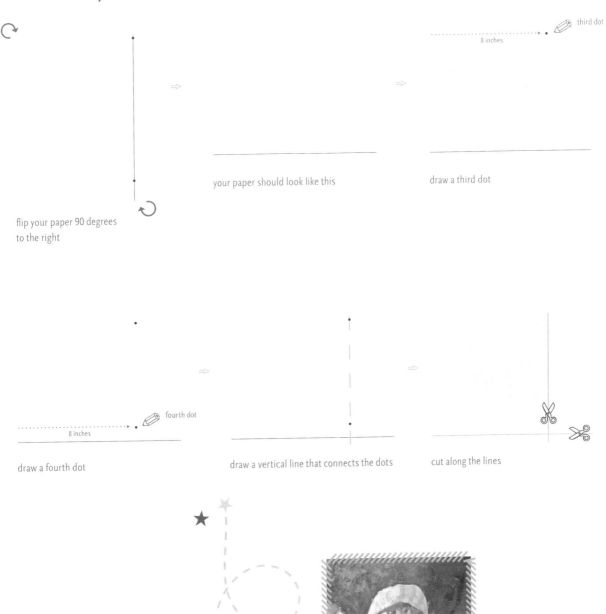

8 inches

third dot

flip your paper 90 degrees
to the right

your paper should look like this

draw a third dot

fourth dot

8 inches

draw a fourth dot

draw a vertical line that connects the dots

cut along the lines

"Now, each of you has an 8" x 8" square in front of you. Your job now is to **divide your individual square up into exact halves**, **quarters** or **eighths**. You must follow the same procedures that you just used to make your initial square and, after careful measurement, you may make your cuts. Note that the shapes of your fractions may end up being squares, rectangles or even triangles, depending on how you decide to divide up your square. The important part though is that you measure carefully and then cut. After you have made your cuts please stop and wait for the rest of us. Given that we have 21 kids, we will need a few additional squares to fill out the quilt. These can be done by anybody who finishes early."

8" x 8" square   examples of possible shapes cut from your square

"Now that we have all cut our squares into various fraction pieces, it is time to **put them all together into a quilt**. I will put the various shapes down on the floor and then everybody in the class may move two shapes to another location in the design. We will do this until everyone has a chance to move two pieces around and we reach consensus on the overall design. When the shapes are in their final pattern, we can cooperatively work to glue them on top of the poster board that has already been cut to the appropriate size. When the shapes are glued and in place we will let it dry and then hang up in our dining car for all to see."

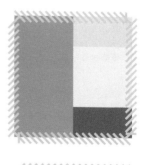

Let's Get it Started
Multiplication Facts

AS WE START OUR STUDY of multiplication and division, I am going to let you in on a little secret. Ready? Come closer. Here it is. The first three rules that you need to know about multiplication are really, really easy. Most people who write math textbooks make a big deal about this and spend many pages explaining it, but since you are all so smart I am just going to tell you straight up. Here are the three things:

ORDER PROPERTY   says that **order doesn't matter when multiplying**.
For example: 3 x 2 = 6   and   2 x 3 = 6

ONE PROPERTY   says that **anything times one equals itself**.
For example: 7 x 1 = 7,   1 x 15 = 15,   12543 x 1 = 12543

ZERO PROPERTY   says that **anything times zero equals... ZERO**!
For example: 7 x 0 = 0,   0 x 12 = 0

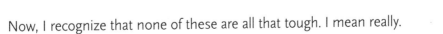

Now, I recognize that none of these are all that tough. I mean really.
You are all saying, "Of course," or "I knew that," or "Well, duh."

Try the following questions on for size and see how you do

1. 3 x 4 =

2. 4 x 3 =

3. 9 x 4 =

4. 4 x 9 =

5. 132 x 1 =

6. 1 x 24 =

7. $\frac{1}{2}$ x 1 =

8. 1 x $\frac{1}{4}$ =

9. 1456 x 0 =

10. 17, 345, 768, 908 x 0 =

11. 1 x 17, 345, 768, 908 =

No sweat eh?

multiplication facts

Let's start our look at multiplication facts by looking at Zero ⇨

zero one two four eight five ten three six nine seven

Zero

Below you will see a number of math facts. Each one has two FACTORS that are multiplied together to reach a product. One of the factors in each of these is a zero. Therefore the product is zero too. We know this from the ZERO PROPERTY that we just learned. After you answer each of these simple equations, look at the products and see if you can find three different patterns. Please write these patterns down the right side of the page. You will be doing this for each of the multiplication facts from 0–9.

*Notice that next to each fact is a star (*).*
Please write down how many facts have a star next to them at the bottom of the page. You will see why later.

Solve the following equations

*   0 x 0 = _____

*   0 x 1 = _____

*   0 x 2 = _____

*   0 x 3 = _____

*   0 x 4 = _____

*   0 x 5 = _____

*   0 x 6 = _____

*   0 x 7 = _____

*   0 x 8 = _____

*   0 x 9 = _____

*   0 x 10 = _____

Name 3 number patterns that you notice

1.

2.

3.

How many facts have stars? _____

1.   Ryan drank zero milk shakes. How many milk shakes did he drink?

2.   Evan slept for zero minutes this afternoon. How long was his nap?

Let's look now at your ones

Remember, all new facts
*have a star next to them (*).*
This will be important later.
For now, just count them.

one

Solve the following equation

1 x 0 = _____

*   1 x 1 = _____

*   1 x 2 = _____

*   1 x 3 = _____

*   1 x 4 = _____

*   1 x 5 = _____

*   1 x 6 = _____

*   1 x 7 = _____

*   1 x 8 = _____

*   1 x 9 = _____

*   1 x 10 = _____

Name 3 number patterns that you notice

1.

2.

3.

How many facts have stars? _____

Fill in the blank below

The _____ says that anything times one equals itself.

For example: 9 x 1 = 9,   23 x 1 = 23,   76001 x 1 = 76001

Now, let's look at your twos

Solve the following equations

2 x 0 = _____

2 x 1 = _____

*   2 x 2 = _____

*   2 x 3 = _____

*   2 x 4 = _____

*   2 x 5 = _____

*   2 x 6 = _____

*   2 x 7 = _____

*   2 x 8 = _____

*   2 x 9 = _____

*   2 x 10 = _____

Name 3 number patterns that you notice

1.

2.

3.

How many facts have stars? _____

Put it to work...

Yesterday, Grace A. went shopping for a new flip'n'flyer. A nice shiny purple one to replace our old beat up classroom one. They were only two dollars each. What a deal!

How much would 2 cost? _____

How much would 3 cost? _____

How much would 7 cost? _____

How about 14? _____

How much would 24,000 cost? _____

Did you include your dollar signs?

What is the pattern here?

Multiplication Facts

OUR TYPICAL CIRCUS DAY starts with a late-night drive into town. Luckily Nancy drives well at night. She follows the "arrows" ··· → ··· → ··· → ··· → posted by the "24-Hour Man," or should I say Person, from the day before. Once we are on the circus lot, and are guided to our parking space, we all get a few hours of sleep before set-up begins first thing in the morning. Set-up is the most grueling aspect of circus life, in which the equivalent of a small town must be erected in the span of only a few hours before the public arrives. The work is divided up into smaller crews who handle the tent, the seating, the electrical generators and wiring, the animals, and the various midway concession stands. All of our performers are responsible for setting up our own rigging at the appropriate time.

Typically there will be one or two performances on set-up day, two performances on weekdays, and three performances on weekends. Immediately following the last show at a particular location, everything is dismantled and packed into trucks, or back on our train, after which everyone hits the road to the next town. We sometimes perform this entire ritual every day ("one night stands"), and of course it goes on regardless of weather, fatigue, or the presence or absence of any paying customers. Luckily, with our fantastic unicyclists, diabloists and jugglers we always have a great crowd!

For more neat info about the circus check out the following web page:

www.circusweb.com

} What did you learn on the web page?

Now, let's look at your fours

Wait. What happened to the threes? Don't worry. They are coming, but only after the tens. Confused? Here is the order: 0, 2, 4, 8, 5, 10, 3, 6, 9, 7. Any idea why? Just keep going and you'll see.

Solve the following equations

4 x 0 = _____

4 x 1 = _____

4 x 2 = _____

✶   4 x 3 = _____

✶   4 x 4 = _____

✶   4 x 5 = _____

✶   4 x 6 = _____

✶   4 x 7 = _____

✶   4 x 8 = _____

✶   4 x 9 = _____

✶   4 x 10 = _____

Name 3 number patterns that you notice

1.

2.

3.

How many facts have stars? _____

So... why do you think that Will loves the number 4 so much? Any guesses?

The first circus ring

One integral part of our circus is the animals. Animal acts have been a real crowd pleaser from the very start of circuses throughout time. In fact, now check this out, the first circus ring was constructed around **the distance it takes four horses to turn a complete circle.** In other words, four horses were strapped together and forced to turn as tight a circle as possible. The circumference that they made was recorded and this length became the basic measurement for the first circus ring. Cool eh?

1 horse 2 horse 3 horse 4 horse

Circus Smirkus

Another great circus is the famed Circus Smirkus in Vermont. It is a very special circus that consists only of children performers. Kids are the clowns, trapeze artists, tumblers and just about every other part of a working circus. Kids spend multiple week long sessions of training before they hit the road and perform all over Vermont for the second part of the summer.

B🤡NUS

• •

For those who are able to log on to their home computer, try to answer the following questions from the Circus Smirkus web page **www.circussmirkus.org**. Good Luck. For trivia points? Maybe.

1.   What city is Circus Smirkus located in?

2.   How much would a diablo cost at Circus Smirkus? How much would four of them cost?

3.   What year did the Circus Smirkus start?

4.   If you had the opportunity to attend a Circus Smirkus camp, would you? Please write a four sentence paragraph explaining why or why not.

_____

_____

_____

_____

_____

_____

_____

Visit the Circus Smirkus website at:

www.circussmirkus.org

• • • • • • •

Will loves number four!

Let's now look at your eights

See, I told you eight was coming next. Let's see... do you notice a pattern yet?

2, 4, 8? Hmm. Read on brothers and sisters, read on.

Solve the following equations

Name 3 number patterns that you notice

8 x 0 = _____

8 x 1 = _____   1.

8 x 2 = _____

✻   8 x 3 = _____

8 x 4 = _____   2.

✻   8 x 5 = _____

✻   8 x 6 = _____

✻   8 x 7 = _____

✻   8 x 8 = _____   3.

✻   8 x 9 = _____

✻   8 x 10 = _____

How many facts have stars? _____ Why is this number decreasing with each new fact?

Try the following questions

1. What is half of eight? _____

2. How many twos go into eight? _____

3. Twice two equals what? _____

4. Four times half of eight equals? _____

5. If I doubled four and then doubled it again, what would my answer be? _____

6. What is $\frac{3}{4}$ of eight? _____ Explain why.

7. If 8 x 3 = 24, what is 8 x 30? _____

8. (8 x 7) – (8 x 2) = _____

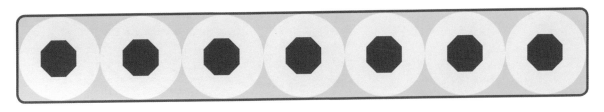

Now, let's look at your fives

Solve the following equations

5 x 0 = _____

5 x 1 = _____

5 x 2 = _____

*   5 x 3 = _____

5 x 4 = _____

*   5 x 5 = _____

*   5 x 6 = _____

*   5 x 7 = _____

5 x 8 = _____

*   5 x 9 = _____

*   5 x 10 = _____

Now how many facts

have stars? _____

Name 3 number patterns that you notice

1.

2.

3.

An
ALMOST
true
story

Skyler J. and Celia built a little circus the other day. They created tiny figures, various pieces of equipment, and tents. Since their circus was so small, they decided to pay their performers in small amounts, like nickels. They decided to pay each of the following performers in our circus the following number of nickels. How much did each performer get in dollars?

Tumblers   *6 nickels =* _____   **Unicyclists**   *34 nickels =* _____

Ringmasters   *8 nickels =* _____   **Jugglers**   *4 nickels =* _____

Clowns   *3 nickels =* _____   **Musicians**   *9 nickels =* _____

Acrobats   *3 nickels =* _____   **Diabloists**   *214 nickels =* _____

YOUR TURN. Choose another form of payment that you think people in our circus would appreciate. Make a chart below that says who the performers are and how they are paid. HAVE FUN!

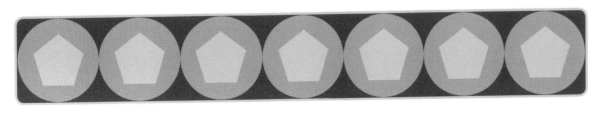

Let's look at the easy one... Tens

Solve the following equations

10 x 0 = _____

10 x 1 = _____

10 x 2 = _____

*   10 x 3 = _____

10 x 4 = _____

10 x 5 = _____

*   10 x 6 = _____

*   10 x 7 = _____

10 x 8 = _____

*   10 x 9 = _____

*   10 x 10 = _____

Name 3 number patterns that you notice

1.

2.

3.

How many facts have stars? _____

The circus was now winding its way through the south, and we reached the great state of Texas. In Texas everything is big, Big, BIG! So big that we all ate ten times as much as we usually do. If Marlena could usually eat 2 hamburgers for lunch, she would eat 20 in Texas. Really! Check out what some of the rest of us ate...

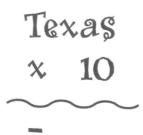

Texas

1.   Alex could usually eat 12 pretzels, but in Texas he ate _____.
2.   Dominic could usually eat 87 goldfish snacks, but in Texas he could actually put away _____.
3.   Nico's daily diet of 145 pickles turned into _____ pickles.

$$\text{Texas} \times 10 = $$

Threes

3 x 0 = _____

3 x 1 = _____

3 x 2 = _____

✻   3 x 3 = _____

3 x 4 = _____

3 x 5 = _____

✻   3 x 6 = _____

✻   3 x 7 = _____

3 x 8 = _____

✻   3 x 9 = _____

3 x 10 = _____

How many facts have stars? _____

Name 3 number patterns that you notice

1.

2.

3.

Try these trees, I mean threes

The Big Apple Circus has a really cool web site. Check out the "intro video" and the "virtual circus" page. They are both really neat.

www.bigapplecircus.org

Let's use some of these 3 facts that you have been studying. In order to go to the circus, one must pay... of course! Let's say that you wanted to go to the Big Apple Circus in New York. On the next page is a chart of how much you might pay to attend the Big Apple Circus. Please use the chart on the next page, and your knowledge of the 3-tables, to answer the questions. ⇨

Multiplication Facts

SEATING SECTION	Center Ringside	Center Box	Ringside	Box	Mezzanine	Grandstand
Peak show prices	$115.	$115.	$105.	$105.	$95.	$65.
Non-peak show prices	$100.	$100.	$95.	$95.	$80.	$50.
11 am weekday matinee	$55.	$55.	$40.	$40.	N/A	$40.

1. Nico wanted 3 ringside seats for a non-peak show. How much did he pay?

2. Would this cost the same as sitting in non-peak box seats?

3. If Brandi took Andrew and Liam to the circus and wanted to sit in the best seats possible, how much would it cost the three of them to go to the circus and where would they probably sit? (Assume that they were going to a peak show.)

4. Ashley decided to take her very good friend Moxie to the circus. They went to a peak show and paid $315. for the 3 tickets. Where could they have sat?

5. Use the chart above to make up two challenging questions, and YES, please answer them as well.

    1.

    2.

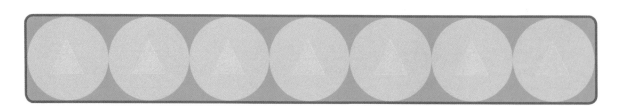

Let's now look at your Sixes

Multiplication Facts

Sixes

Solve the following equations

6 x 0 = _____

6 x 1 = _____

6 x 2 = _____

6 x 3 = _____

6 x 4 = _____

6 x 5 = _____

* 6 x 6 = _____

* 6 x 7 = _____

6 x 8 = _____

* 6 x 9 = _____

6 x 10 = _____

Name 3 number patterns that you notice

1.

2.

3.

How many facts have stars? _____

Here are a couple more web sites
to keep you busy

www.wisconsinhistory.org/circusworld
www.surfnetkids.com/circus.htm

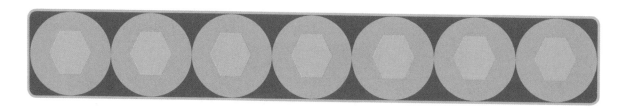

Multiplication Facts

Let's now look at your nines. We are almost finished...

Solve the following equations

9 x 0 = _____

9 x 1 = _____

9 x 2 = _____

9 x 3 = _____

9 x 4 = _____

9 x 5 = _____

9 x 6 = _____

⁎ 9 x 7 = _____

9 x 8 = _____

⁎ 9 x 9 = _____

9 x 10 = _____

Name 3 number patterns that you notice

1.

2.

3.

How many facts have stars? _____

Let's look some more at the patterns that we see in the nine's tables. Complete the following table and notice all the patterns.

9 x 3 = 27	2 x 7 = _____	2 x 1 = _____	3 x 7 = _____
9 x 4 = 36	3 x 6 = _____	3 x 1 = _____	4 x 6 = _____
9 x 5 = 45	4 x 5 = _____	4 x 1 = _____	5 x 5 = _____
9 x 6 = 54	_____	_____	_____
9 x 7 = _____	_____	_____	_____
_____	_____	_____	_____

Now that you have filled in the table, please list 5 patterns that you notice

1.

2.

3.

4.

5.

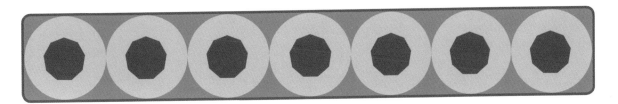

Naughty Number Nine

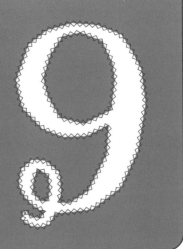

Please write a detailed paragraph on the infamous circus clown **Naughty Number Nine**. The requirements for your paragraph are as follows: Naughty Number Nine must be the main character, and she must have three friends who are all named various multiples of nine such as 27, 45 and 81. Naughty Number Nine must somehow be nasty and it must all take place at our circus. Oh yeah, one more thing: it must be in cursive. **Have fun**.

_____
_____
_____
_____
_____
_____
_____
_____
_____
_____
_____
_____
_____
_____
_____
_____
_____
_____
_____

Finally, let's look at your sevens

Solve the following equations

7 x 0 = _____

7 x 1 = _____

7 x 2 = _____

7 x 3 = _____

7 x 4 = _____

7 x 5 = _____

7 x 6 = _____

* 7 x 7 = _____

7 x 8 = _____

7 x 9 = _____

7 x 10 = _____

Name 3 number patterns that you notice

1.

2.

3.

How many facts have stars? _____ So tell me, why are we down to only one star?

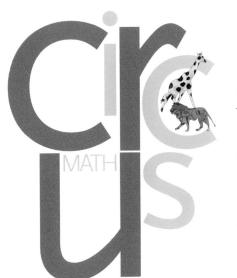

So, is that it? Are we finished multiplication yet? Hardly. These first pages on multiplication were simply a look at the multiplication facts and how we might use them in our circus. Knowing these facts and how to use them is just the start of multiplication fluency. We still need to look at some more vocabulary, factoring and mental math in order to make our circus successful. So what are we waiting for?

But wait... look at this extra space!

Hmm. How about trying the following?

1.   4 x 3 − 2 + 5 = _____

2.   9 x 6 + 14 − 23 = _____

3.   50 x 20 − 75 + 25 = _____

4.   97 − 99 + 4 + 98 = _____

5.   50 x 20 x 10 − 900 = _____

6.   (7 x 1) + (6 x 3) = _____

7. $\frac{1}{2}$ + 4 − 3 = _____

8.   42 − 49 = _____

9.   (18 − 3) x 8 = _____

10. $\frac{1}{4}$ + $\frac{3}{4}$ − $\frac{1}{8}$ = _____

Last one, Ready? 126 is also a very special number. Why?

Feeding the Troupes
Multiplication Project

7

EVERY ONCE IN A WHILE, our circus train needs to stop and pick up supplies. As you can imagine this is a very big deal as we need supplies for all of our 21 performers, our driver Nancy, our numerous helpers, and of course our teachers and animals. As we were driving through Oklahoma, Kansas and Nebraska, we stopped at a local Giant Foods store to buy groceries.

Will's Grocery List

bread
milk
cereal
rope
Band-aids
tennis balls

— *Here is what was on my list to buy*

Now, I knew that I needed a lot of stuff, so I decided to help organize myself and make a chart before I left for the market. Good thinking, but some of the values on my chart rubbed off in my pants pocket. Poor me ☹. Luckily, I have worked hard on my fractions and place value and can fill the blank places in myself.

123456789101112

Here is my chart. Please help me by filling in any blanks. Then please use the completed chart to answer a few questions.

Will's Grocery List

ITEM	bread	milk	cereal	rope	Band-aids	tennis balls
Quantity	10 loaves	50 gallons	200 boxes	50 feet	_____ boxes	12 cans
Cost	$1.50 a loaf	$3.00 a gallon	_____ box	$10.00 a foot	$7.00 a box	$3.00 a can
Total Cost	$ _____	$ _____	$400.00	$500.00	$14.00	$ _____

1. If I bought $\frac{1}{2}$ as many loaves of bread, how much would they cost instead?

2. If a can of tennis balls has three balls in it, how much would seven balls actually cost?

3 What if I decided to buy 6 yards of rope? How much would this cost?

4. Many of our fourth grade circus stars love cereal. How much would they pay for 300 boxes of it?

5. Which would cost more, 5 boxes of Band-Aids or 10 cans of tennis balls?

Finally, make up four problems of your own using the data from the chart.

6.

7.

8.

9.

In our travels we will see many
new people, cultures and traditions

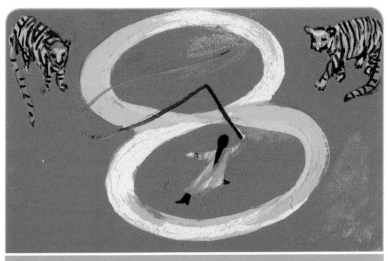

Life on the Road
Multiplication Concepts and Skills

VOCABULARY

Now it is time to look into some vocabulary words that will help you in your continued understanding of multiplication and division. Some of these we have already talked about and some are new. Take a look at a few very important multiplication related vocabulary words.

FACTOR   **A number that when multiplied with another factor equals a product.**
For example: if one takes the two factors 4 and 3 they
are multiplied to get the product of 12.   4 x 3 = 12

PRODUCT   **The answer one gets when two factors are multiplied.**
2 x 5 = 10. Ten is the product of the two factors 2 and 5.

SQUARES   **When a number is multiplied by itself, it is a square.**
For example: 2 squared is 2 times itself, or 2 x 2, which obviously
equals 4. Or 4 squared equals 16, or 12 squared equals 144... Get it?

PRIME NUMBER   **A number that has only two products, one and itself.**
For example: 7 is prime, yet 8 is not because it has
four factors: 1, 2, 4 and 8.

1234567891011112

Multiplication Concepts and Skills

1. Nico says that the product of 3 and 6 is 18. Is he right? Prove it.

2. The product is 40. One factor is 10. What is the other factor?

3. One factor is 50 and the product is 200. What is the other factor?

4. The next prime number after 11 is...

5. If two prime numbers are multiplied together, is there product prime? *Be careful...* Explain your answer.

6. What is 9 squared?

7. The product is 240. Give me 4 different equations with 8 different factors that have the product of 240.

Please make up three of your own questions using the multiplication vocabulary and then answer them. Try to make them an appropriate challenge instead of ridiculously easy. Thanks.

✳ FACTOR
✳ PRODUCT
✳ SQUARES
✳ PRIME NUMBER

8.

9.

10.

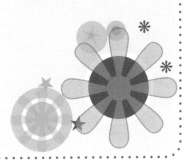

Mental Math Quickie

Now try these problems in your head. Remember to multiply the first digit in each number and then add the appropriate number of zeros to your answer. Remember that the answer in a multiplication problem is called a PRODUCT.

1. 40 x 300 = _____

2. 30 x 600 = _____

3. 80 x 70 = _____

4. 300 x 4000 = _____

5. 80 x _____ = 240

6. _____ x 50 = 1000

7. 4 x _____ = 120

8. 60 x _____ = 4200

Multiplication Concepts and Skills · · · · · ·

The day the CLOWNS CRIED

Not all days in circus history have been filled with laughs. The saddest day in circus history has long been considered the day of the great fire in Hartford Connecticut, July 6, 1944. Take a minute and read all about it, and then we will use the information to look at a few new kinds of problems.

ON JULY 6, 1944 A FIRE BROKE OUT during a Ringling Brothers performance in Hartford, Connecticut. One hundred sixty-seven people died as a result of the blaze, which broke out while several thousand were under the big top for an afternoon performance. Flames spread instantly along the canvas of the tent since it had been waterproofed with a mixture of gasoline and paraffin. The spectators' stampede to escape proved as deadly as the fire; hindering the escape of many were steel railings along the front of the bleachers and an animal chute blocking a main exit.

The circus fire remains the worst disaster in circus history. Because it was a circus performance, and because it occurred on a Thursday afternoon during World War II, when many adults held down one or more jobs at war-production plants, children accounted for many of the casualties. Only 100 of the dead were older than 15. The injured numbered 487. The lot where the circus performed—bounded by Barbour Street, Cleveland Avenue, Hampton Street and Kensington Street—became the site of the Stowe Village housing project.

Just a few things for you to think about... and yes, answer below.

1. How many people died in the Great Hartford Fire?

2. How many people were injured?

3. Why did the fire spread so quickly?

4. Do you think this kind of fire could ever happen again? Why or why not?

_____

_____

_____

_____

_____

_____

_____

_____

_____

Now that was intense. Never before or since has such a horrific event occurred. After the fire, many people got together to review how the tragedy happened and what they could do to avoid repeating their mistakes in the future. The material used to make and coat the tents was changed, emergency exits were always kept open, and the number of people allowed at any event had to meet very strict fire codes. All of these safety measures were put into place so that going to Ringling Brothers or any other circus can be an enjoyable as well as safe experience for all children.

Setting up Multiplication Problems

Now that we have looked at some new vocabulary and the various patterns involved in each of the multiplication facts, we are ready to set up multiplication problems. It is really important, though, that you understand the value of each digit in any given number. For example:

How much is the 4 worth in the number 48? _____

If you said 4, try again. The 4 is actually worth 40 because it is in the tens column or place. How about the 8? Since the 8 is in the one's place, it is worth 8. Get it? Try a few yourself.

If my number is 456

My 4 is worth _____   my 5 is worth _____   my 6 is worth _____

If my number is 7,398

My 9 is worth _____   my 3 is worth _____   my 8 is worth _____

Last one...
*   Be careful*

If my number is 34,908

My 3 is worth _____

my 9 is worth _____

my 0 is worth _____

What did you say the zero was worth?
Did you say zero, ten or seven?
IF you said ten,
you are wrong.
IF you said zero,
you are right.
IF you said seven...
you are crazy.

thousands   hundreds   tens   ones

Let's start with simple problems that have two digits multiplied by one digit. We have done a number of these already, so this should be a review. Make sure, though, that the two problems are lined up correctly from the start, because as the problems get more difficult you will definitely need things to be in neat columns.

1.   21
       x 4
       _____

2.   23
       x 3
       _____

3.   63
       x 5
       _____

4.   78
       x 2
       _____

multiplication

5.   67
        x 6

6.   81
        x 9

7.   40
        x 9

8.   99
        x 2

9.   67
        x 3

Now, I would like you to write up exactly what you did. For example, look at the following problem:

24 x 8 =

If I wrote this problem out it might look like this ⇩

- First I look at my one's column and see that in my one's column I have an 8 and a 4.
- I multiply the 8 and the four and get 32.
- I carry the 3 (putting it above the 2) and put the 2 in the one's place of my answer.
- Then I multiply the 8 by the 2 in the tens place and add the 3 that I had carried giving me a total of 19, which I put in the answer to the left of the 2.
- My answer is 1 9 2, which of course is one hundred and ninety two.

Glad you don't have to do that every time eh? Yeah, me too. You do have to do it two times, though, because I am basically mean. Set these up, solve them the regular way, and then write out exactly what you did. You will thank me for this when you get to fifth grade.

Try this one:

76 x 4 =

OK, secret number 245. Are you ready?

. . . .

When you add more digits to a multiplication problem all you do is continue the same pattern. Let's repeat that.

When you add more digits to a multiplication problem all you do is continue the same pattern. Let's repeat that.

So if you are multiplying 356 times 17, don't freak out about the 1, just continue the pattern until you run out of digits to multiply. How cool is that and I did not even make it up.

Set these up and try them. *Don't forget to carefully line up your columns.*

1. 345 x 33 =

2. 632 x 73 =

3. 902 x 58 =

4. 917 x 47 =

Did the zero mess you up in problem 3? I hope not. Just multiply the 8 times the zero, get zero, and add the one that you had carried. You are so smart!

Food and the Circus

. . . .

One of the many important elements of the circus is food. Max and his family spend a great deal of money on food while we are traveling around the country. Here are a few examples of the kinds of problems he had to do while there to make sure that he had enough money to pay for all that he needed.

One day in Utah (we had recently left Colorado) Max bought the following items:
3 candy bars at $2.50 each, 2 drinks at $3.00 each and one peanut butter and jelly sandwich at $6.00.

Please answer the following questions

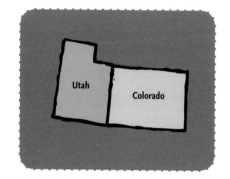

- How much did he spend on his candy bars?

- How much did he spend on his drinks?

- Were his three candy bars more or less expensive than his sandwich?

- Finally, how much did he spend in all?

Now it is Dominic's turn. Wow is he a big eater.

Though we had moved west into Arizona, Dominic wasn't interested in the traditional foods of the many native American tribes from that region. The delicious flat breads with cheese or chicken and beans were of little interest to him. Instead, he ate mostly junk food. He bought 7 slushies at $5.00 each, 2 hamburgers at $7.59, 9 balls of cotton candy at $2.75, and finally she ate... for dessert... 8 large cookies at $9.45 each. Them some expensive cookies.

- How much did Dominic, I mean his dad John, spend on the hamburgers?

- Which cost more, the hamburgers or the cotton candy?

- Finally, John paid for Dominic's food with a $100 bill. What was his change?

One more

After a particularly difficult practice one day, Ryan went into the local town to find a place to eat. He came across a beautiful diner, which happened to also be empty. He bought 6 sandwiches and 8 drinks that day. How much did he spend if the sandwiches cost $5.00 and the drinks cost $2.50 each?

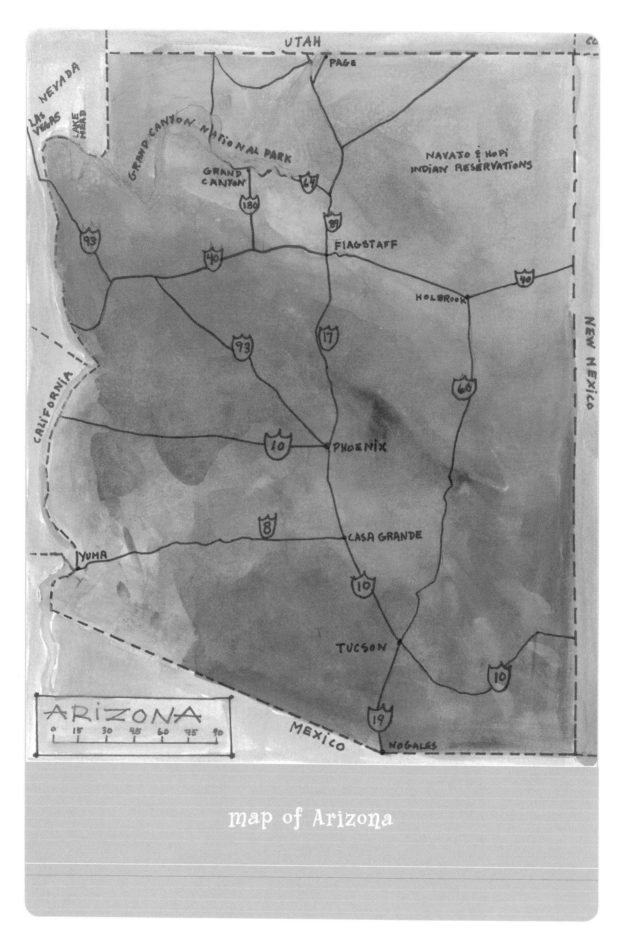

map of Arizona

Fine, Fine, Fine. All of that is fine, but what about using it in our circus?

For this section we are going to talk to another very important person in our circus, our transportation coordinator Nancy. Nancy is in charge of making sure that all the people, animals and gear actually get where they need to be each and every day of our tour. When I approached Nancy, she was talking on the phone while looking at a map of Arizona. She was probably planning the details of how we will get to our next stop. But as I was listening, Ace and his motorcycle family were practicing, so a few of Nancy's words could not be understood. Maybe you can help me out by filling in the blanks in her dialogue. Obviously, feel free to use the map of Arizona.

CIRCUS MATH MAP

Arizona

Nancy's dialogue:

"Well, we are finishing up with two big shows in Tucson on Friday. From here we will drive up I-10 to Phoenix. Driving at the reasonable highway speed of 55 mph, it should take about _____ hours to get from Tuscon to Phoenix. From there we better take interstate _____ to get up to Flagstaff for the afternoon performance. And hey, look at what National Park is just north of Flagstaff. Maybe some of the circus kids would like to visit _____.
If we drive all the way west through the park, we will arrive in the state of _____ and soon be in Las Vegas for our evening show. This is perfect as interstate _____ can then be taken southwest to reach the truly great state of _____. Wow, that is a very long day. By the end of it we will have traveled roughly _____ miles. (pause) Yes, I think we can do it. See you Sunday."

(Isn't it amazing how timely Ace's family was with their motorcycles? I am so glad that you are here to help me fill in some of the blanks.)

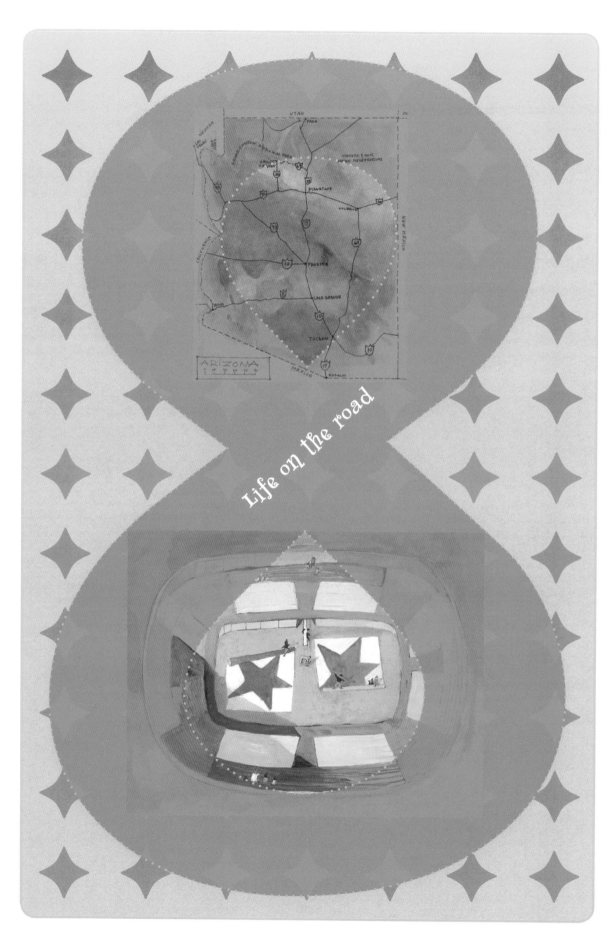

Life on the road

And on to... California

What a state. Just like in Arizona, we are really busy. Below, I wrote a short list of just few things we need to do. Read carefully...

> - Buy 20 bags of dog food. Each bag weighs 40 pounds.
> - Each of the 75 gallon water tanks needs filling. Fill each of the three tanks.
> - Grace A's high wire walking family needs more wire. Buy 25 of the 1000 foot spools.
> - Rebuild Nico's death defying trampoline landing pit. We need 720 feet of lumber to do the job.
> - Take out the trash. All 123 bags of it.

What a list. That's a lot of math. Let me think. I have some questions to figure out. Imagine that. ☺

1. How many pounds of dog food do I need to buy in all?

2. I will need _____ gallons to fill all of the _____ tanks.

3. Poor Nico. His platform really needs to be fixed. (Ouch). He can fit 240 pieces of lumber in our truck at a time. How many trips will he have to make to bring all the lumber that poor Nico will need?

4. The 123 bags of trash were generated in just three days. That would be approximately how many bags in a week?

5. Finally, how many feet of wire does Grace A. need?

BONUS BONUS BONUS

▼ ▼ ▼ ▼ ▼ ▼ ▼ ▼ ▼ ▼ ▼ ▼ ▼ ▼ ▼ ▼ ▼ ▼ ▼

These are optional, but you never know.... *Ok, smarty pants. Try these if you dare.*

1. Roughly how many miles of wire are actually needed?

2. If lumber comes in eight foot lengths, how many lengths are in 720 feet?

3. One out of every three bags of trash (hey, that is a fraction, $\frac{1}{3}$ of the bags of trash) are generated by the clowns. How many bags of trash would this be?

4. The nozzle to our hose is broken and is only letting in 5 gallons a minute. How long will I be standing by the three tanks in order to fill them all?

5. If each of the 40 pound bags of dog food costs $10.00, how much would I spend for 20 bags?

▲ ▲ ▲ ▲ ▲ ▲ ▲ ▲ ▲ ▲ ▲ ▲ ▲ ▲ ▲ ▲ ▲ ▲ ▲

As we drove towards California, Andrew was quietly relaxing with a book about the _____ state. He read that California has many large cities. The three largest are _____, _____ and _____. Wow, he thought, and none of these are its capital, which is _____.

Andrew also read up on some California history. He learned that in 1849 many people came to California to look for _____. He also discovered that only one US president was born in California. It was none other than _____.

Finally, Andrew discovered that as we drive north out of California we will be heading directly into the great state of _____. Now that looks like a really cool place to live, he thought. With these thoughts he drifted off to sleep. After all, life at the circus is very busy.

As Ace drifted off to sleep, he had a very strange dream. In his dream he was putting on his makeup for our upcoming show at the Portland Rose Garden. Suddenly, his friends came running into his dressing room asking him strange multiplication questions. With your help, maybe he can answer them.

Nico: Hey Ace, what is 245 x 34?

Skyler J: Hey Ace, what's the product of 1876 and 49?

Suddenly, the breaks of the train squealed and Ace woke up right as we pulled into our next destination... the ⇨

Portland Rose Garden arena! One of Ashley's many jobs at the circus is to handle ticketing. Take a look at the map of the Rose Garden and see if you can answer just a few of the many types of ticket issues that Ashley has to deal with at each stop.

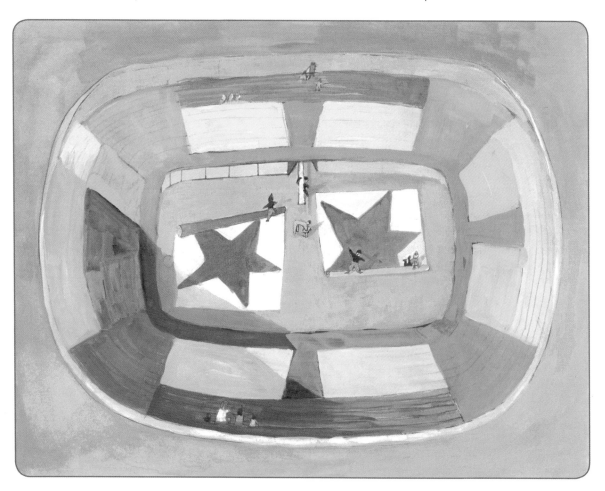

map of Portland Rose Garden arena

1. Franklin High School wants to bring 300 students and 20 teachers to our afternoon performance. They will each need to buy a 12 dollar ticket. How much will they be spending in all?

2. Ockley Green Middle School wants to sit only in the yellow sections. The reason is that their principal, Jackie Bidney, loves the color yellow. If each of the six yellow sections holds exactly 350 people, how many people can they bring in all?

3. Finally, Stephenson Elementary School wants to come and see the circus. Given that they are friends with Ashley, they get special seats right on the floor of the arena. They will be sitting in 12 rows of 28 people in a row. How many seats will they need in all?

We are now some 2,800 miles away from Plymouth Meeting Friends School and about to begin the final leg of our journey back East. With our spirits high and our skills continuing to grow, our circus is thriving. We better get a moving, though, as we have a few more stops to make, and we need to be back in the Steinbright Building for our first performance on our home turf.

. . . .

And now ladies and gentlemen...

Welcome to division

Goin' Down the Road
Division Concepts and Skills

LISTEN UP EVERYONE. Remember that when we first started our journey into multiplication we worked on all of those multiplication facts? We looked at each fact, worked on memorizing them and how to use them in various equations? Do you remember? Since then we have traveled half way around the country and learned how to use these facts in a variety of problems and situations. Good for you!

The really cool thing is that as we move into division, you have already learned much of what you need to know. Really! Would I lie to you? You see the division facts are only the INVERSE to the multiplication facts. Inverse? What does that mean? It means that **division is really the opposite of multiplication** and therefore you are already off and running. Let me show you why.

If 4 x 3 = 12, then 12 ÷ 3 = 4 and 12 ÷ 4 = 3

IF that isn't amazing enough, it is true with all multiplication fact families.

If 8 x 2 = 16, then 16 ÷ 2 = 8 and 16 ÷ 8 = 2

● ● ● ● ● ● ● ● ● ● ● ● ● ● ● ● ●

123456789101112

Try these

If 5 x 3 = 15,   3)‾15‾ = _____ and   5)‾15‾ = _____

If 8 x 7 = 56,   8)‾56‾ = _____ and   7)‾56‾ = _____

One more:
If 4 x 6 = 24,   4)‾24‾ = _____ and   6)‾24‾ = _____

Many members of our circus troupe know how to juggle. Those who are learning how to juggle are working with three balls, and the real experts can juggle up to eight balls. Many members are working on other combinations between three and eight balls.

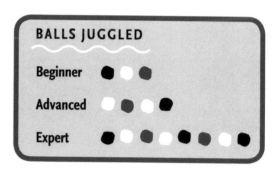

BALLS JUGGLED

Beginner

Advanced

Expert

Let's look at a few different situations:

1 beginner would need _____ balls
3 beginners would need _____ balls
8 beginners would need _____ balls
12 beginners would need _____ balls

Let's look at the inverse of these situations:

3 balls could be used by _____ beginner juggler
9 balls could be used by _____ beginner jugglers
27 balls could be used by _____ beginner jugglers

If I found 17 balls, how many beginner jugglers would have enough balls? _____
How many would be left over? _____. (That number is called the REMAINDER!)

Yesterday two of our expert jugglers, Nico and Evan were cleaning up from our last performance in Washington State. They decided to juggle with apples, and, well, it got a little messy. As a result they switched back to juggling balls. They saw a big bag of 24 juggling balls. They were thinking about the number 24 and realized that 24 could be divided into many different sized groups. Can you write down no less than six different fact families that involve the number 24? These can be either multiplication or division facts.

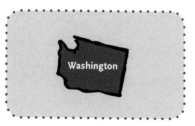

Washington

1.   3.   5.

2.   4.   6.

As you can see, we need a lot of balls to keep our jugglers happy, no matter how much experience they have. Now, try to answer the following questions!

1. If Nico is an expert juggler, how many balls will he need?

2. If both Moriya and Dominic are advanced jugglers, they will need how many balls to practice?

3. Thirty six balls can be divided evenly by how many advanced jugglers?

4. Our juggling bag holds 66 balls. Remembering that jugglers with more skill need more balls, what is the greatest number of jugglers who can perform simultaneously from each of the three categories?

These juggling balls are all stored in small wooden boxes on the jugglers' train car.
Each box holds up to 24 juggling balls.

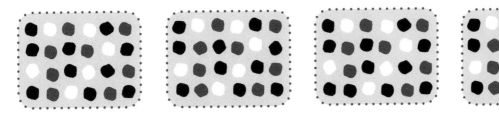

four small wooden boxes on the jugglers' train car

-   Given this, how many beginners can juggle with one full box of balls?

-   How many advanced jugglers can juggle with one full box of balls?

-   Finally, how many experts can juggle with one full box of balls?

WE BUNDLED UP, presented our passports and crossed the American/Canadian border to travel north to the Canadian city of Edmonton, home to the Edmonton Oilers' hockey team.

The class arrived just in time to catch a performance of the **National Circus School**. The troupe had traveled 2981 kilometers (as they say in Canada) or 1852 miles from their home in Montréal in the province (similar to our state) of Québec.

We marveled at the acrobats, and afterward we enjoyed a cup of hot chocolate with the Premier of the Province of Alberta (he's the Ring Master for government, with a job similar to that of our state governors).

But with home 2013 miles away, it was time to say bonne nuit or good night and all aboard for the final leg of our journey.

To learn more about the Canadian National Circus School visit:

www.nationalcircusschool.ca

Can you name a Canadian province that begins with the letter "O"?

_____

The
Province of Alberta

WELCOMES

The Fourth Grade Class

to a

PERFORMANCE

of

THE *nationalcircusschool*

TRAVELING SOUTHEAST TO MINNESOTA, we had a number of smaller performances. In this land of over 12,000 lakes, we seemed to be performing in a variety of settings which called

for a great deal of setting up and taking down. One of the smallest venues that we performed at was in the small town of Stillwater, MN. We were asked to set up only **four dozen** chairs for this performance, as the space was quite limited. Grace E., Mimi, Marley and Celia each grabbed some chairs and started the setting up process. Since the school's gym had a small stage on one side of the gym, they decided to use the stage and to set up the seats in straight lines in front of the stage.

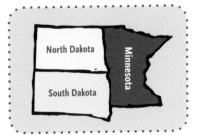

Let's listen in on their conversation

⇩

You may draw the chairs how ever you wish

Grace E.: "I think that we should set up all the chairs in 2 rows of 24 chairs right in front of the stage. In this way all of the seats are close to the stage. If I were to draw it, it would look something like this."

stage

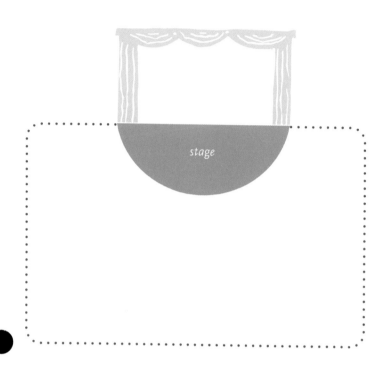

Mimi: "No, no, no Marley. In your set up people will be way off to the sides. I think we should have 8 rows of _____ which would give us our required _____ seats. Look, I'll draw it for you."

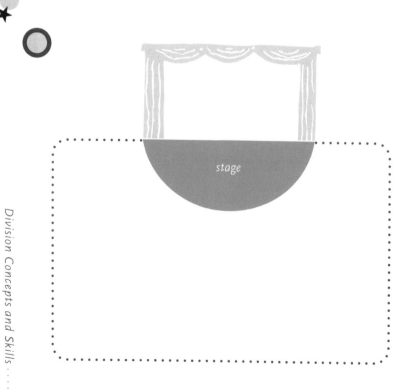

Marley then spoke and said: "No, no no Celia. That has too many rows and many of the kids will be too far back from the stage. I think we should have _____ rows of _____. Look, I'll draw it for you."

After Marley spoke, all eyes were on Maya. *Grace E. asked Celia,* "Well, what do you have to offer?" *Then Mimi said,* "Yeah, you've been awfully quiet", *and Marley chirped in saying,* "Yeah, what you got, and don't say 1 row of 48 people either."

Celia: "Well, you have all given good suggestions, but I would still do it differently. I would have _____ rows of _____ kids which would get us exactly to our goal of 48 students and teachers. See, here is my drawing."

stage

THE
RETURN
OF

Naughty
Number
Nine

$9 \times 5 = 45$ $45 \div 9 = 5$ $45 \div 5 = 9$

VOCABULARY time

As we continue to talk about divison, we need to build a vocabulary to talk about three important new vocabulary words. They are: DIVISOR, DIVIDEND and QUOTIENT.

DIVISOR **The number that is divided into a dividend to get a quotient.**
For example: $4\overline{)8} = 2$ and $8 \div 4 = 2$

4 is the *divisor* in both problems.

DIVIDEND **The dividend is divided by a divisor to get a quotient.**
For example: $18 \div 6 = 3$ and $6\overline{)18} = 3$

18 is the *dividend* in both problems.

QUOTIENT **The quotient is the answer to a division problem.**
For example: $45 \div 9 = 5$ and $9\overline{)45} = 5$

5 is the *quotient* in both problems.

All good circus performers know these terms and can use them with $\div$ or $\overline{)}$
In other words...

The dividend ÷ the divisor = the quotient

$$\text{The divisor}\overline{)\,\text{the dividend}}^{\text{quotient}}$$

1. Moxie says that if the divisor is 4 and the dividend is 16, then the quotient is 4. Is she telling the truth?

2. Alex told me as he was practicing his unicycle that if the dividend is 56 and the quotient is 8, that the divisor must be 7. Is he right as well?

3. True or False. The dividend is always higher than the quotient. *Please explain your answer.*

4. Celia likes the number 10. Can you make up a division problem where the number 10 is used for both the quotient and the dividend. Feel free to write it down both ways... please.

5. $7 \overline{)140}$ = ? Moxie says the quotient is higher than 17 and lower than 24. What could it possibly be?

6. Finally, Moriya found two small cards on the floor. One was a 15 and the other was a 60. The third card completed the division fact family, but she was not able to read it. (Tristan had run over it with his motorcycle.) What was this final number?

Dividing larger numbers

❶ **Divide**

❷ **Multiply**

❸ **Subtract**

❹ **Bring down and repeat**

Let's start with a few problems that use these four steps. Try them yourself and then we'll review them together. Remember if the problem uses a ÷ symbol, you need to re-write the problem with a $\sqrt{}$ before solving it.

Good luck.

1. $5\overline{)26}$

2. $3\overline{)17}$

3. $14\overline{)18}$

4. $7\overline{)43}$

5. $13 \div 6 =$

6. $75 \div 15 =$

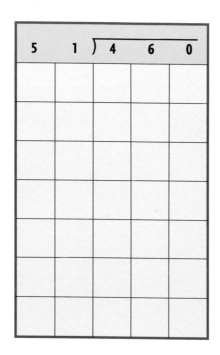

How did those go? Did you remember to write the remainders down next to your answer? If not, please go back and do so now.

When you are doing problems with even larger numbers all you need to do is to repeat those four steps until you have solved the problem. *Let's do this one together.* I have put it in a grid to help you align the digits while solving the problem.

Not bad eh. Did you remember the remainder? Are you sure that is has one?

Finally, try these last two by yourself. Remember **D, M, S, B.**

1.   6) 7805

2.   14) 1696

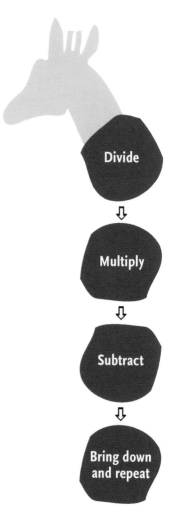

Division and multiplication

Don't try these at home. Actually, do try these at home!

1. 16 ÷ 2 =

2. 12 x 3 =

3. 24 ÷ 4 =

4. 100 ÷ 20 =

5. 8 x 7 =

6. 40 x 20 =

more ⇨

7.   15 x 3 − 5 + 10 =   8.   63 ÷ 9 + 7 =

9.   If each of Minnesota's 12,000 lakes had exactly 4 fish in each lake, how many fish would there be in all?

five of Minnesota's 12,000 lakes

10.   56
     x 89
    ――――

11.   204
     x 76
    ――――

12.   1197 ÷ 3 =

13.   329 ÷ 12 =

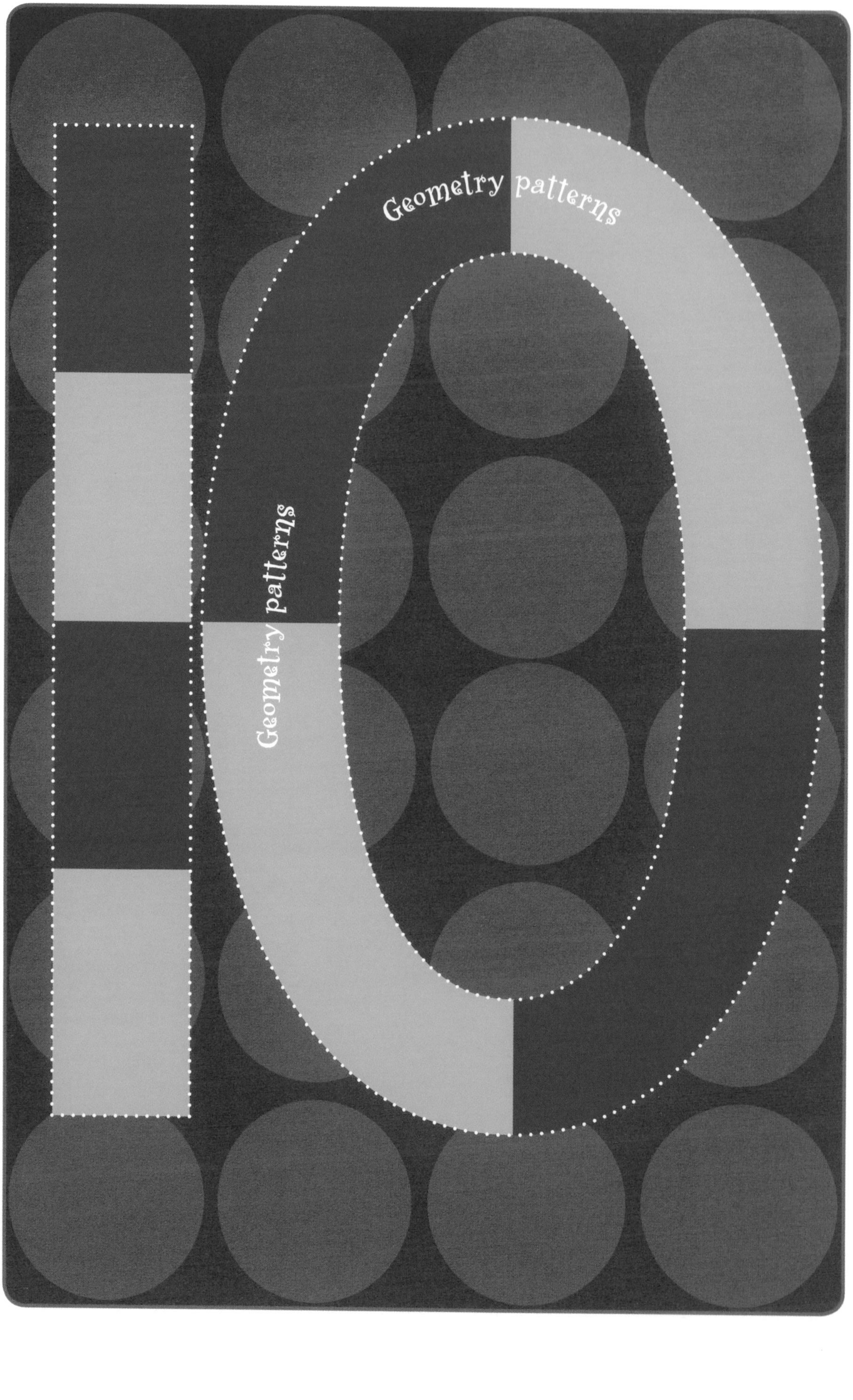

Geometry patterns

Geometry patterns

Don't be Square, Dude
Geometry

BACK ON THE ROAD. Though it has been a wonderful journey, we are all getting a bit tired and ready to wrap up our trip. A few more stops and we'll be heading back home to our comfortable beds, home cooked meals and our parents. Just as Will was drifting into a reflective state, Jesse knocked on the door.

"Come in" Will said pleasantly.

"Hey Will ... I have a question. A few of us were looking at the manual for installing the new trapeze and it said that the guide lines need to be perfectly parallel. What does parallel mean anyway?"

"Good question Jesse. How about I show you?"

"Parallel and perpendicular lines are an important concept that all of you need to understand as we jump into our study of geometry. Now, come follow me."

Will and Jesse walked over to the area where the trapeze kids had been busily working. Will asked all of the kids to follow him as the group went to the outside of the train car and literally climbed up onto the top of our speeding train. (Remember that this is Will that we are talking about ☺)

Parallel and Perpendicular

Will then calmly asked all the kids to sit quietly in the breezy air. As we nervously sat there Will asked us to look out at the railroad tracks in front and in back of the train. These two track lines are PARALLEL. They will never intersect or cross. As the train continued down the tracks we noticed that this was true, they remained exactly the same distance apart, never getting any closer or farther away from each other. Even when the rails turned towards the right, or left, they stayed exactly the same distance apart.

parallel lines

Then Will said, "PERPENDICULAR lines
on the other hand
cross at a 90 degree angle.
They cross like two roads, or like a

_____."

"I get it" Skylar S. said.

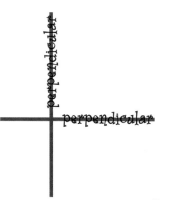

perpendicular lines

"Great, Will replied. Now can you name
2 examples of *parallel lines* that we have in the circus?
1.

2.

"How about 2 examples of *perpendicular lines*?"
1.

2.

"Very cool. Good job. As you can see it is really important for those trapeze lines to be exactly parallel so that the bar itself hang parallel to the floor. How about you all climb down safely, go finish your project and meet me in the dining car for a little lunch."
Eager to get off the top of the train we obliged and enthusiastically went to finish our project.

Volume and Area

Meanwhile, in another train car, Brandi and Liam were slowly gathering their belongings and trying to pack some of their clothes. After a brief chat about their wonderful adventures together, they realized that they were having a hard time squeezing all of their stuff back in their suitcases. Here is how the conversation went:

Brandi: "Hey Liam, I think my suitcase shrunk"

Liam: "No it didn't, you have simply added more stuff during our journey. The volume of your clothes and personal belongings has grown during our journey.

Brandi: "Maybe the volume of my suitcase got smaller?"
(giggling)

Liam: "Actually, the volume of your suitcase has stayed the same. You see, VOLUME is the amount of space that something occupies. It is a *three dimensional measurement*. The volume of your suitcase has stayed exactly the same, yet the volume of things that you have put it has grown.

Brandi: "Oh, I get it!"

Liam: "That new CD player that you bought in Memphis, those cowboy boots that you purchased in Lubbock, TX and even those beautiful earrings that you got in Santa Fe all take up volume in your suitcase."

Brandi: "So...what then is area and how is it different from volume?"

Liam: "Oh, that's easy. AREA is a particular section of a *two dimentional*, or flat, surface. So, you might talk about the area of a piece of paper, such as our circus tickets, or the area of our ceiling parachute.

Brandi: "Cool, that makes sense"

Liam: "Just to be sure that you really get it...try these. I am going to give you examples of things that we use in our circus and you tell me if it is measured in Volume or Area? Ok? Here we go..."

this inside bit is the area

Liam's Questions

1. Our storage cars are measured in _____.

2. The floor surface of our next performance is measured in _____.

3. Our ticket size if measured in _____.

4. The _____ of our food car is larger than my car.

Liam: "Well done, you really got it! Now, in order to reduce the volume of things in your suitcase, you must take out a few things such as that beautiful blue... sweater. Hey, that's mine."

Brandi: "Sorry. Let's go get something to eat before the big meeting this afternoon. I am starving"

Liam: "You got it."

Let's go get something to eat before the big meeting this afternoon

Angles

Today we will learn a bit about angles. All angles are divided into one of four categories. They are either acute angles, right angles, obtuse angles and a straight angle.

A RIGHT ANGLE measures **exactly 90 degrees**. The two lines that make this angle are parallel. One example of this is seen on our trapeze. The angles between a trapeze and the ropes that hold it up are 90 degrees, or a right angle.

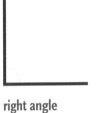

right angle

Please draw a trapeze and mark the 90 degree angles on it.

An ACUTE ANGLE is anything **between 0 degrees and 90 degrees**. We see these angles all over our circus. Can you tell me two places that we see them?

1.

2.

acute angle

An OBTUSE ANGLE is anything **greater than 90 degrees**. Where do we see these in our show? Tell me two of them?

1.

2.

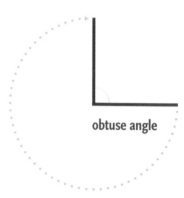

obtuse angle

Please draw a Circus Scene on the page to your right.

The scene must have the following geometrical elements included in the drawing:

☐ 2 Right Angles
☐ 2 Acute Angles
☐ 2 Obtuse Angles
☐ An example of Area

☐ An example of Volume
☐ Parallel Lines
☐ Perpendicular Lines

Geometry

AS THE TRAIN MOVES swiftly across the Appalachian Mountains and into our home state of Pennsylvania I look up at the clock to see that we are due to arrive back at the station in only a few hours. Looking at the hands of the clock I realize that the hands make an angle. For example, when it is exactly 3:00 the two hands make a 90 degree angle and when it is 4:10 the hands make a 60 degree angle. Thinking this is pretty cool I think of ways to use a regular clock to show my circus stars the connection between clocks and angles.

Excitedly I think of an idea and run to talk to some of them.

I ran into a small group of kids who were still in the dining car. They had finished their lunch and were exchanging their e-mail addresses when I approached enthusiastically. I asked if they had ever thought about the angles that are made by the hands of a clock? As they looked at me strangely, I walked over to the wall and took down the car's clock. I set the time to both 3:00 and 4:10 and explained about the 90 degree angle concept.

Then I gave them these times and asked what angle they made?

1.   2:00   _____

4.   7:00   _____

2.   9:00   _____

5.   6:00   _____

3.   10:35   _____

Now try these...

Please solve using >, < or =

The angle made by the hands of a clock at 3:00 is _____ the angle at 9:00.

The angle made by the hands of a clock at 2:15 is _____ the angle at 12:10.

The angle made by the hands of a clock at 4:05 is _____ the angle at 7:45.

Give me three different times where the angle made by the hands of the clock is exactly 90 degrees.

1.

2.

3.

Perimeters

As the train started to slow down Will gathered us all together for one last lesson. Figures! He wanted to teach us a little bit about perimeters. The lesson went like this.

Will: Does anyone know what a perimeter is?

Mimi: I do. A PERIMETER is the measured distance around a flat object.

Will: Very good. Can you give me an example?

Mimi: Sure. My bongo board is 24 inches long and
         12 inches across. If I add the four sides together
         I get a perimeter of 72 inches.

Will: Excellent. Now can everyone else look at their
         math books and find the perimeter of the
         math book cover?

         PLEASE MEASURE THE
         PERIMETER OF YOUR ACTUAL
         MATH BOOK COVER!

MATH BOOK COVER PERIMETER = _____

Will: Now, look for two other flat objects that you have been using in the circus and,
         in the spaces on the following page, draw the objects and label the length
         of each side as well as the overall perimeter.

draw
the objects and label the
length of each side
as well as the
overall perimeter

As we finished our drawing we began to hear the train breaks squeal. We knew we were home...

The Big Clean Up
General Review & Measurement Project

AS THE ENGINES PULL OUR TRAIN BACK into 30th Street Station, in Philadelphia, we are collectively proud of our accomplishments and extremely tired from our journey. As people start to greet families and friends who have come to greet us, we reminisced about our experiences and time in the circus. Our entourage then got on the bus and made our way back to school. After we unloaded all of our gear Will reminded us that we had one more really important responsibility as a group—we needed to clean up. After the usual complaints, most kids sat down and waited for instructions on how to get this last job done. Here is what he said:

> " Before we all go home, we have one last project to do. Each tour we go through hundreds of rolls of paper towels as we clean up our trains, equipment and cages. This year I want to try a little experiment and actually test some of the different kinds of towels to see if we are really getting our money's worth. I have divided you up into four groups and each group has a separate test to try on each of the towels. When we have all had a chance to test each of the towels, we'll compare our findings and reach consensus on which towel we feel is the best. The categories that we'll be testing for are strength, absorbency and cost. As a group you will also think of one more category to judge your towels. All of the equipment that you need has been put on your tables so now we can start. ⇨

12345678910**11**12

STRENGTH

PERSONAL
TOWEL STRENGTH RANKING

Towel A _____

Towel B _____

Towel C _____

Towel D _____

❶ Gather enough paper towels so that each member of your group has one of each brand. Get each wet and ring them out. Then have each member of your group "clean" your chosen surface and evaluate which of the towels seems to be the strongest.

Record your information in the box ⇦ at left

GROUP
TOWEL
STRENGTH
RANKING

_____   _____
strongest   ⇨   weakest

❷ After everyone in your group has done their own cleaning and recording of data, please discuss your results with each other and come up with a group ranking of the four towels, from strongest to weakest and record it in the box at left.

_____

_____

_____

_____

_____

_____

_____

_____

❸ Finally, write a brief paragraph about your experiment.

Please include where you did your experiment, what you discovered and ultimately what the group's results were.

ABSORBENCY

❶ Gather enough paper towels so that your group has one of each brand. Decide on how your group plans to test for absorbency and do the same test for each towel. You are going to record your group information in the box at right.

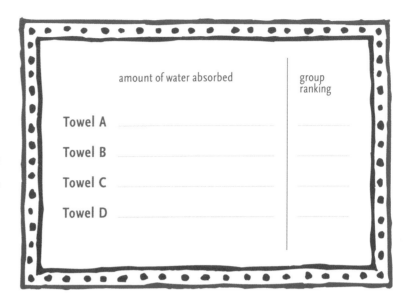

amount of water absorbed   group ranking

Towel A ....

Towel B ....

Towel C ....

Towel D ....

❷ After your group has tested each towel, please rank your towels. They should be ranked from the most absorbent to the least absorbent.

TOWEL ABSORBENCY RANKING

most absorbent ⇨ least absorbent

❸ Finally, write a brief paragraph about your experiment.

Please include how you tested for absorbency, if you had any surprises that you encountered while doing your experiment and what your group discovered about the four towels.

COST

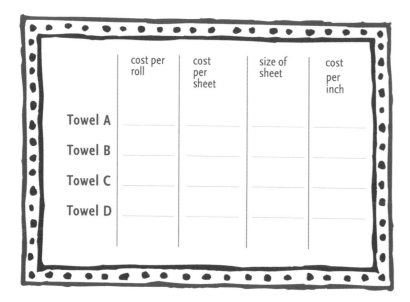

	cost per roll	cost per sheet	size of sheet	cost per inch
Towel A				
Towel B				
Towel C				
Towel D				

❶ Gather enough paper towels so that your group has one of each brand. Your group may use calculators to fill in the grid below. I will give you the cost of each roll as well as the number of sheets that came on your roll. From this information you must measure the size of each sheet and write that on the chart. Then you must calculate the cost per square inch of each towel and put that information in the final column.

TOWEL
COST
RANKING

most expensive ⇨ least expensive

❷ After your group has ranked each towel, please record your information.

❸ Finally, write a brief paragraph about your experiment.

Please include if you had any surprises that you encountered while doing your calculation and what your group ultimately discovered about the four towels.

FINAL CATEGORY = _____

❶ For the fourth and final experiment, we need to collectively decide one other way to evaluate and test our sample of paper towels.

❷ After we reach a decision each group will conduct their own experiment and record the information in the box at right.

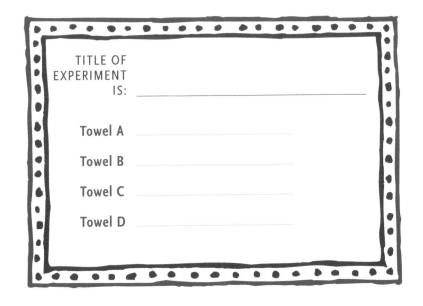

TITLE OF EXPERIMENT IS: _____

Towel A _____

Towel B _____

Towel C _____

Towel D _____

❸ Now, please write a **detailed description** of the whole experiment. Include information on how the class decided on a topic, how your group tested for it and what you discovered about the four towels.

_____

_____

_____

_____

_____

_____

_____

_____

_____

_____

_____

FINAL RESULTS OF OUR BIG CLEAN UP

After all of the experiments are completed we will gather once again as a group and fill in this final grid with all of the information that we collectively gathered. From this information we will be able to give a final overall ranking of the four chosen towels. Only after that will I reveal the actual brand name of each towel.

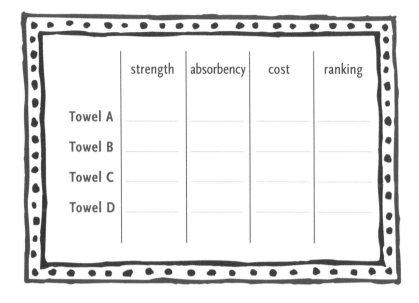

	strength	absorbency	cost	ranking
Towel A				
Towel B				
Towel C				
Towel D				

We'll compare our findings & reach consensus on which towel we feel is the best

wrap up QUESTIONS

1. Which towel was ranked the highest in our experiment?

2. Did this surprise you in any way?

3. Was the most expensive towel worth the extra money?

4. Does this change the brand of paper towel that you will use at home?

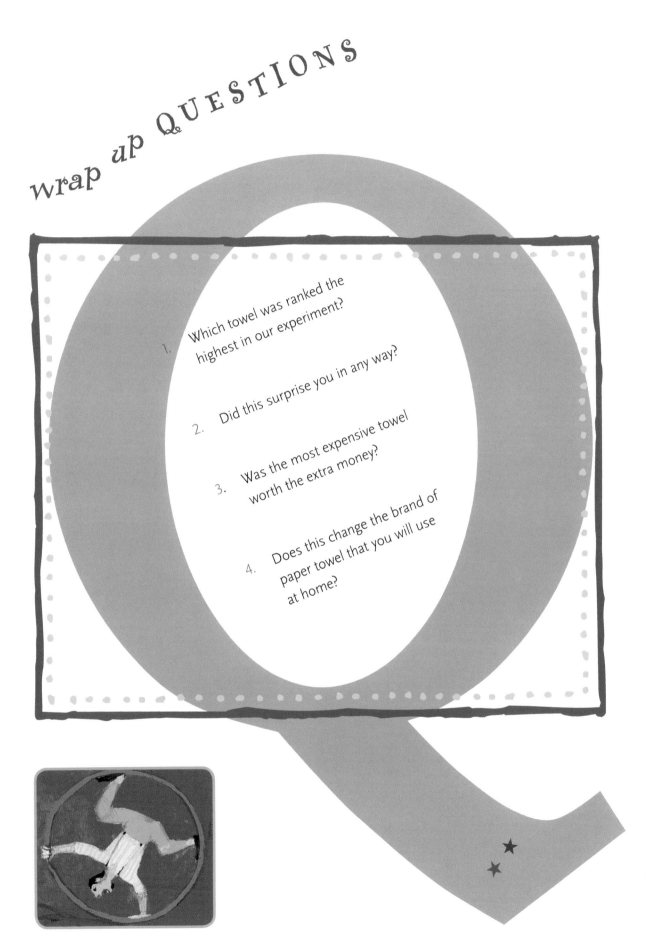

Wrap it Up
Conclusion

WELL, I GUESS THIS IS REALLY IT. It is finally time to say our last goodbyes and for the kids to go home. We gathered one last time in our classroom when Will and Ashley got our attention and spoke to the group. This is what Will said:

66 I would just like to say a few words to all of you before you scatter and go back to your homes. I would first like to thank the parents for their support in this year long journey and for their efforts to help bring our circus alive. From the work you did before our journey even began, building sets and finding sponsors, to the emotional support and guidance you gave your kids while on the road, it truly could not have been done without you. I would also like to thank Ashley for her continued help and support in this endeavor and hope that we will have many more such journeys in the future. Finally, I would like to thank the 17 of you. Throughout the last nine months you have worked hard to master new skills, think up exciting routines and work together to put on a series of remarkable performances. I am so proud of each of you for what you have brought to this circus and this class. I wish you all a wonderful reunion with your families and many enjoyable evenings as you recount and share some of your many adventures. All the best.... 99

And with that we all got our things, filled up our family cars and drove home. It had been a wonderful trip, one that I will never forget. Even the math. ☺

123456789101112

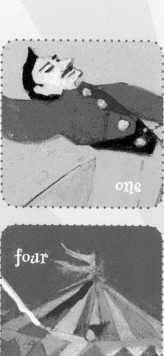
one

two

three

four

five

six

seven

eight

nine

ten

eleven

twelve

4207794

Made in the USA
Charleston, SC
13 December 2009